Lighthouse Accommodation
Britain and Worldwide

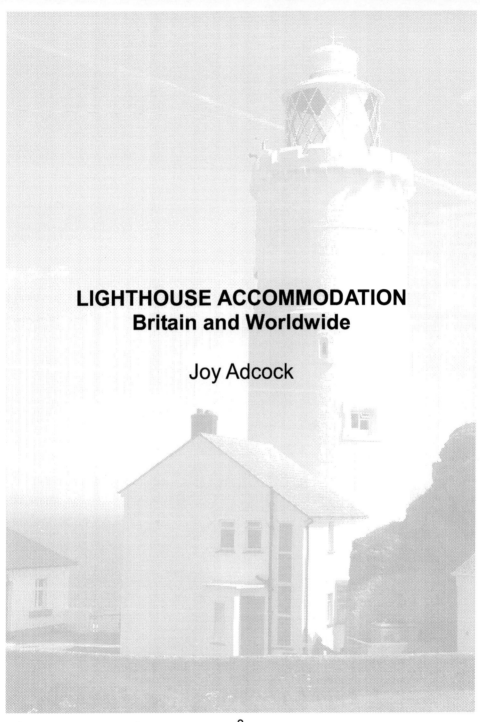

LIGHTHOUSE ACCOMMODATION
Britain and Worldwide

Joy Adcock

Written and published by Joy Adcock,
23 Aldis Road, Acle, Norwich NR13 3BN

First Edition published March 1999 by Joy Adcock
0 9535182 0 5

Second Edition published May 2001
Reprinted January 2003
0 9535182 1 3

Third Edition published April 2008
Fourth Edition published January 2009
978 0 9535182 2 7

The information contained within this book is correct to the best of
the author's knowledge. Every attempt has been made to contact
the owners of properties listed. The author and publisher accept no liability
for any errors or omissions within this book.

All photographs by Joy Adcock & Patrick Tubby
unless otherwise specified

Front cover: Start Point Lighthouse, Devon

Back cover:
Pot a l'Eau de vie (Canada): photo byLa Société Duvetnor,
Cape Otway (Australia): photo by Paul Thomson
Lynmouth Foreland, West Usk (UK)

CONTENTS

INTRODUCTION

South Stack, Anglesey

Perhaps like many lighthouse enthusiasts (pharologists), my interest stems back to childhood holidays. My first visit to a lighthouse was South Stack Lighthouse in Anglesey at the age of 9, when I was able to climb the tower, look round the lantern and marvel at its workings. I can still vaguely remember crossing the perilous bridge which connected the tiny island to the mainland, and climbing the endless steps up the zigzag pathway back to the car.

I can also recall visiting Start Point Lighthouse in Devon when 12, staying on holiday in the village of Strete, and this is really where my passion began. My parents told me that I used to ask them to stop the car on the way back from wherever we had been that day so that I could sit and watch the beams flashing out to sea. I remember being woken early one morning by the familiar moan of its foghorn.

My first stay in a lighthouse was in 1994 at Great Orme's Head Lighthouse in Llandudno, a disused lighthouse which had been converted into a Bed and Breakfast. During that stay I was able to re-visit South Stack Lighthouse, but this time it was not open to the public, and the bridge across to the island was closed. Now thankfully it is once again open.

Since that time I have stayed in a number of lighthouses, both in the UK and abroad.

In this book, the history of each of the UK lights is not intended to be comprehensive; some have vast histories which would need a separate book of their own, and I have therefore tried to maintain a balance by giving where possible, equal coverage to each lighthouse. I hope that I have provided a taste of each unique building.

Britain's lighthouses are now all automated, and missing the human element, save the occasional visits by the attendant or maintenance staff. As a result of automation the cost of running a lighthouse has been reduced significantly, and whilst the initial expenditure of the automation process was high, within a few years most of this could be recouped. Advances in technology and the use of natural resources, such as solar power have further helped to reduce running costs. Lighthouses are funded by light dues, charged to commercial shipping. Automation and the cutting of costs has ensured that light dues have remained frozen for the past few years, and this continues to be reviewed.

When Britain's lighthouses became automated, the lighthouse authorities of Trinity House (England and Wales) and the Northern Lighthouse Board (Scotland and the Isle of Man) no longer had use for the majority of the keepers' dwellings. Many lighthouses became inaccessible to the general public, but now thankfully a number have re-opened, providing holiday accommodation in former keepers' cottages and visitor centres. This will ensure that the buildings continue to be used and therefore preserved, and perhaps give a flavour of what it would have been like to live the life of a lighthouse keeper.

With the advances in satellite technology, radar and other navigation equipment, the need for lighthouses, particularly for commercial shipping, is diminishing. Modern technology is the way forward, making navigation safer. It is another phase in our maritime history. For mariners lighthouses are still invaluable, providing above all some degree of reassurance.

Most of the lighthouses in this book are still operational, though some have been discontinued and sold off to conservation organisations. These lighthouses were built to last and to withstand the elements. I hope they will continue to do

so. The human element will never be forgotten in the courage of the engineers and keepers who often risked their lives for the sake of others.

Please visit them, enjoy your stay, and help to keep our maritime history alive.

Joy Adcock

ACKNOWLEDGEMENTS:

I would like to thank the following for their assistance with this book:

Chris Dodson (Trinity House), Lorna Hunter (Northern Lighthouse Board), Gerry Douglas-Sherwood (Association of Lighthouse Keepers), Esbjörn Hillberg (Swedish Lighthouse Society), Keith Morton, Frank Turner, Roy Thompson, Lin Sunderland, National Trust for Scotland, Christine Steenfeldt and Katie Wilsdon (Rural Retreats), the owners of their accommodation and everyone else who has helped to make this book possible.

Most of all I would like to thank Patrick Tubby for his patience, support, enthusiasm and attention to detail.

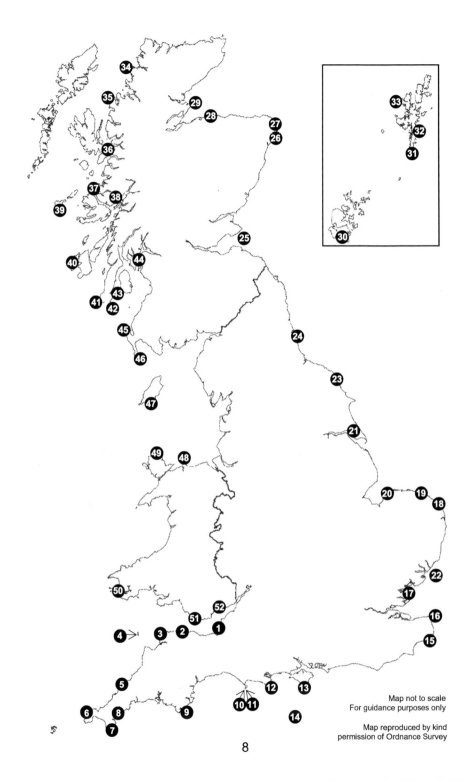

Map not to scale
For guidance purposes only

Map reproduced by kind
permission of Ordnance Survey

8

UK LIGHTHOUSES

1. Burnham Old High Light, Somerset
2. Lynmouth Foreland, Devon
3. Bull Point, Devon
4. Lundy Island, Bristol Channel
5. Trevose Head, Cornwall
6. Pendeen, Cornwall
7. Lizard, Cornwall
8. St Anthony, Cornwall
9. Start Point, Devon
10. Portland Old High Light, Dorset
11. Portland Old Low Light, Dorset
12. Anvil Point, Dorset
13. St Catherine's, Isle of Wight
14. Alderney, Channel Islands
15. South Foreland, Kent
16. North Foreland, Kent
17. Lightvessel No 15, "Trinity", Essex
18. Happisburgh, Norfolk
19. Cromer, Norfolk
20. Hunstanton, Norfolk
21. Paull, East Riding of Yorkshire
22. Patricia Voyages
23. Whitby, North Yorkshire
24. Souter, Tyne and Wear
25. Isle of May Low Light, Fife
26. Buchan Ness, Aberdeenshire
27. Rattray Head, Aberdeenshire
28. Covesea Skerries, Moray
29. Tarbat Ness, Highland
30. Cantick Head, Orkney
31. Sumburgh Head, Shetland
32. Bressay, Shetland
33. Eshaness, Shetland
34. Stoer Head, Highland
35. Rua Reidh, Highland
36. Eilean Ban, Highland
37. Ardnamurchan, Highland
38. Corran, Highland
39. Hynish Signal Tower, Tiree
40. Loch Indaal, Argyll and Bute
41. Mull of Kintyre, Argyll and Bute
42. Sanda, Argyll and Bute
43. Davaar, Argyll and Bute
44. Toward Point, Argyll and Bute
45. Corsewall Point, Dumfries and Galloway
46. Mull of Galloway, Dumfries and Galloway
47. Langness, Isle of Man
48. Great Orme's Head, Conwy
49. Point Lynas, Isle of Anglesey
50. St Ann's Old Higher Light, Pembrokeshire
51. Nash Point, Vale of Glamorgan
52. West Usk, Newport

1 | BURNHAM OLD HIGH LIGHT, SOMERSET

Self-catering cottage, incorporating lighthouse tower, sleeps 6

Contact:
Lighthouse Holiday,
Berrow Road, Burnham-on-Sea,
Somerset TA8 2HN
Tel: 0797 098 3245
www.lighthouseholiday.com

In the 1700s around two thousand boats used the River Parrett each day to load and unload cargo from Bridgwater Bay. Their route was surrounded by treacherous sand banks.

On a stormy night in 1750, legend has it that a sailor's wife lit a candle in the window of her home at Burnham-on-Sea to guide her husband's ship home. After hearing about this, local seamen agreed to pay the woman to keep the light burning. Realising that money could be made, a local curate, Reverend Davies, and the Church Sexton were sent to buy the business from the woman for £5. She died a wealthy widow. A beacon on the roof of the St Andrews church tower was lit by the Reverend. Later a four storey round tower was built next to the church, becoming the first lighthouse in Burnham. This tower is still in evidence today, although it is no longer used as a lighthouse.

In 1813 Reverend Davies negotiated a 100 year lease with Trinity House to continue his commercial enterprise. In return he paid them £135 per year. The remaining 85 years of the lease was bought back by Trinity House In 1830 and Reverend Davies received £13,681 17s 3d.

Joseph Nelson was asked by Trinity House to design and build Burnham High Lighthouse, and later also designed the Low lighthouse on the beach. Whilst building the High Light, it is said that one labourer fell to his death, and his ghostly moans are still heard on stormy nights.

After the High Light was completed in 1830, it was found that too low a vantage point had been selected to take into account the massive rise and fall of the tides, so a wooden lighthouse on legs was built in 1832 to complement the tower. The Low Light was inactive from 1969 until it was re-established on 31st December 1993. The light on the Low Light is shown through a window at the front, is painted white with a single vertical red stripe on its front face and is 29ft tall with a conical roof and mounted on nine timber pilings. It remains an active aid to navigation and is visited by many thousands of walkers every year. The High Lighthouse also has a red stripe, which when aligned with the Lower light,

forms a useful transit by day, guiding ships safely into the channel.

Burnham High Lighthouse became a semi-watched light in the 1920s, this led to the full-time keepers being replaced by a part-time attendant. Their cottages and much of the surrounding land was sold off by Trinity House to become private dwellings. The light was discontinued on the same evening the Low Light was re-established in December 1993. The following year the High Lighthouse was sold by Trinity House and bought by a member of the Rothschild family, in a sealed bid. In 1996 the 110ft High Lighthouse was put up for auction by the Rothchilds. A young journalist Patrick O'Hagan was dispatched to find a story about the auction, but the lighthouse didn't sell. So he obtained the keys and went to see it for himself. He fell in love with the lighthouse, and he and his fiancée Jill Berryman bought the lighthouse.

In a severe gale and snow storm on 2nd March 1897, the SS *Nornen*, a Norwegian barque, lost its anchorage in the shelter of Lundy Island. The wooden boat, her crew of eleven men and the ship's dog were swept upstream onto the mud flats and sandbanks of Brean to the north of Burnham. The local lifeboat pulled the crew and dog to safety, but the vessel foundered. Remains of the wreck can still be seen today.

Accommodation is available in the tower of the High Lighthouse, which comprises eight floors. There are 120 steps to the top of the tower, with the top floor lantern room reached by a steep ladder.

A small pathway leads through the sand dunes to the Low Light, which is located on the beach.

Established: 1830
Height of tower: 33 metres
Discontinued: 1993
Access to tower: Available to guests

Self-catering cottage, sleeps 10: three twin, two double.
Note: Lighthouse is approached by a steep winding drive, and steep steps lead down to the accommodation.

Contact:
National Trust Holiday Cottages,
PO Box 536, Melksham,
Wiltshire SN12 8SX
Tel: 0844 800 2070
Email: cottages@nationaltrust.org.uk
www.nationaltrustcottages.co.uk

Lynmouth Foreland, or Foreland Point as it is sometimes known, is situated two miles to the north east of the picturesque village of Lynmouth on the north coast of Devon. Countisbury Common to the east of Lynmouth starts a clifftop walk to the Foreland, Devon's most northerly point. A service road reaching 1,000ft above sea level leads through the picturesque valley to the lighthouse. The cliffs on the western edge of the common are said to be the highest in England, and the views from the Foreland look out into the Bristol Channel.

The lighthouse, along with its cottages, is built on terraces carved out of the hillside. Access from the service road is by a flight of 58 steps to the first level, not for the fainthearted! Although the squat white tower is only 49ft high, it has an elevation of 220ft above high water spring tides.

On 28th September 1900, the Trinity House Visiting Committee reported that everything was "in readiness for the exhibition of the light". The lighthouse was then officially opened, and on their same visit to the West Country, Pendeen lighthouse in Cornwall was also inaugurated. Lynmouth Foreland was established as a further aid to navigation in the Bristol Channel, 20 miles east of Bull Point, near Ilfracombe.

Its character is four white flashes every 15 seconds. At one time the light had an intensity of 1,000,000 candle power, and a range of 26 miles, but this has now been reduced to 18 miles.

The fog signal, although originally proposed with the lighthouse's construction, was built later, and adjoined the tower on the north side below the lantern, sounding three blasts every 30 seconds. It has since been discontinued.

The station was electrified in 1975 when diesel generators were installed to provide power. In 1986 the lighthouse was connected to the National Grid by the laying of underground cables, the generators were retained to provide emergency power.

Automation came to Lynmouth Foreland in 1993, when Principal Keeper Norman Grindle and Assistant Keepers Leslie Peers and Avery Aish finally left the station on 2nd November, leaving behind 93 years of manned service. The expense of automation was estimated at £78,000, but the running costs were estimated to fall from £111,000 to £28,000 a year. Upon automation, control and monitoring of the light was transferred to the Trinity House Operations Control Centre at Harwich in Essex.

The holiday accommodation is available on the upper floor of the two storey building. A long corridor runs the length of the building, connecting all the rooms. Access to the tower is sealed off. A wall surrounds the buildings, which are listed as being of Special Architectural and Historic Interest. There is a small courtyard at either end of the main dwelling but it should be noted that there is no garden, and the cliffs outside of the perimeter walls fall steeply to the sea below, children should be supervised at all times.

Established:	1900
Height of tower:	15 metres
Elevation of light:	67 metres
Automated:	1993
Character:	4 white flashes
	every 15 seconds
Range of light:	18 miles
Fog signal:	None
Access to tower:	None

| 3 | BULL POINT, DEVON |

Four Self-catering cottages:
>one sleeps 2, one sleeps 4, two sleep 5

Contact:
Rural Retreats,
Draycott Business Park, Draycott,
Moreton-in-Marsh, Glos GL56 9JY
Tel: 01386 701177
Email: info@ruralretreats.co.uk
www.ruralretreats.co.uk

The North Devon villages of Woolacombe and Mortehoe are inseparably linked, with Mortehoe being the much older settlement, and having a dramatic history of wreckers and smugglers. The tapering headland of Morte Point is renowned both for its wild beauty and its treacherous sea conditions. Seafarers were warned to 'avoid the race and rocky ridge of Morte Point' and well they might, for twice daily the incoming tides swirl furiously around the dreaded Morte Stone, a sunken reef of rocks separated by a deep channel from the Point itself. Numerous ships have foundered on the rocks along this coast, five in the winter of 1852 alone. Many people believe that the word Morte means 'death', and legend has it that the Normans christened it the 'Death Stone', although Mortehoe probably means 'stumpy', referring to the shape of the headland.

Many sayings reflect the awe felt about the area: 'Morte is the place which heaven made last and the devil will take first'. The inhabitants, too, gained the reputation for fierceness and their neighbours from Woolacombe were said to come to the village in groups 'because of Mortemen'.

The headland of Morte Point with its Mortehoe Slates is in contrast to the headland of nearby Baggy Point. Designated a site of Special Scientific Interest, it has one of the few surviving examples of coastal heath in North Devon. During the Second World War both the Stone and the Point were used as target practice from land, sea and air.

Near to the village of Mortehoe, Bull Point Lighthouse guides vessels navigating off the north Devon coast with a red sector light marking the Rockham Shoal and the Morte Stone.

A light was first established in 1879 at Bull Point, and operated without undue incident for 93 years, until on 18th September 1972, the Prinicipal Keeper reported ground movement in the area of the engine room and the passage leading to the lighthouse, and that fissures were opening up. In the early hours of Sunday morning, 24th September, 50ft of the cliff face crashed into the sea and a further 50ft subsided steeply, causing deep fissures to open up inside the boundary wall. Walls cracked and the engine room and fog signal station partly collapsed, leaving it in a dangerous condition and putting the fog signal out of action. The lighthouse tower was also deemed unsafe. Later the same day a lighted buoy was placed off the point to provide a navigation light; this was later replaced by a lattice tower placed on the headland. This old light tower was borrowed back from the Nature Conservancy Council who were using it as an elevated hide, it had been given to them previously by Trinity House when the nearby Instow Lights were renewed. The lighthouse optic was installed in the temporary tower, and a lightvessel was placed offshore to provide a fog signal

until a temporary building was erected to house the three diaphone fog signals

A new lighthouse and Principal Keeper's dwelling (see left) were built at Bull Point at a cost of £71,000, and were officially opened in July 1975 by the Deputy Master of Trinity House, Captain D S Tibbits. The lighthouse was designed and built so that as much equipment as possible from the old lighthouse could be reused as it only dated from 1960. The optic was installed in its third site at Bull Point, and much of the fog signal equipment was also reused.

The lighthouse is now controlled and monitored from the Trinity House Operations Control Centre at Harwich in Essex. The fog signal was discontinued in 1988.

The lighthouse is sited on the hill above the holiday cottages, three of which are housed in the 1870s terrace of dwellings (see below), the fourth cottage is the detached 1970s bungalow. There are extensive lawned areas within the complex, however beyond the perimeter walls the cliffs fall steeply to the sea below, children should be supervised at all times.

Established:	1879
Current tower:	1975
Height of tower:	11 metres
Elevation of light:	54 metres
Automated:	1975
Character:	3 white flashes every 10 seconds
Range of light:	20 miles
Fog signal:	None
Access to tower:	None

4	LUNDY OLD LIGHT, BRISTOL CHANNEL

Self-catering: Lower flat sleeps 4,
Upper flat sleeps 5.
Adjacent cottage sleeps 1.
Note: Minimum 2 nights stay, must correspond with sailing or helicopter schedule.

Contact:
The Landmark Trust, Shottesbrooke, Maidenhead, Berkshire SL6 3SW
Tel: 01628 825925
Email: bookings@landmarktrust.org.uk
www.landmarktrust.org.uk

Lundy (Norse for "Puffin") Island, is situated in the mouth of the Bristol Channel, 11 miles out from the north Devon coast. It is 3 miles long and ¾ mile wide. The highest point of the island affords good views of England, Wales and the Atlantic. It was the haunt of Vikings, Normans, pirates and outlaws. With the increase in shipping, piracy flourished, and Lundy became an ideal base for stashing away illicit goods.

The island is formed of granite, and surrounded by 20 miles of dangerous rugged coastline, which makes approaches from either side of the channel difficult. Several bad tidal streams lurk around the island, including the White Horses to the north east and the Hen and Chickens to the north west. It is not surprising therefore that, being right in the centre of these dangerous currents, many lives were lost at sea. In a Royal Commission Report of 1859, it was reported that, between 1856 and 1857, the eastern side of the island found 97 vessels damaged or lost and 44 lives lost. On the western side, 76 ships were lost and 58 lives claimed.

In 1786 a group of Bristol merchants offered to build and maintain a light on the island at their own expense. The foundations for the first light were laid in 1787 on Chappel Hill, later to become known as Beacon Hill, but the project was abandoned shortly afterwards.

In 1819 Trinity House obtained a lease for the light for 999 years and work began again on the same site. The lighthouse was built by Joseph Nelson, and designed by Daniel Asher Alexander, Consultant Engineer to Trinity House. Alexander was one of the best known architects and civil engineers of his time, and designed the lighthouse at South Stack on Anglesey in 1809. He was also responsible for the construction of Dartmoor Prison in 1820.

The lighting mechanism was operated by clockwork, which had to be rewound at regular intervals throughout the night. Two lights were exhibited; one in the main lantern room and one 30ft below. In 1829 an innovative revolving light was installed as the main light. The lower light had a fixed white light shining out to the west, which was designed to be seen at a short range of about 4 nautical miles. If this light disappeared the vessel was too close, but from 5 miles away the upper and lower lights appeared to merge into one.

Because of its high elevation, the light was often obscured in mist and fog, so two Georgian 18 pounder cannons were placed at the base of the tower. These were later moved nearer to sea level to a purpose built fog gun battery on the west side of the island. In another attempt to combat the fog, another lantern room was built at the base of the tower and used if the main light was shrouded in fog. This too, was often obscured and the lighthouse was finally abandoned in 1897, becoming a daymark when two new lights were constructed by Trinity House Chief Engineer Thomas Matthews at the north and south ends of the island.

In 1969 the National Trust took over the island, and many of the buildings were restored. Lundy is now financed and administered by the Landmark Trust, which is an independent conservation charity specialising in the rescue and restoration of historic or interesting buildings, letting them afterwards to finance future maintenance.

Accommodation is provided in the original lighthouse keepers quarters attached to the old lighthouse; a separate cottage within the complex was the former lighthouse keepers' store. Access to Lundy Island is via scheduled boat from Ilfracombe or Bideford, or by helicopter from Hartland Point. Stays on the island have to be coordinated with the helicopter or boat schedules. Facilities on the island are sparse, with one shop and the hospitable Marisco Tavern, but the walks, scenery and relaxed atmosphere are wonderful.

Photo: Landmark Trust

Established:	1820
Height of tower:	29 metres
Discontinued:	1897
Access to tower:	Available to guests

| 5 | TREVOSE HEAD, CORNWALL |

Four self-catering cottages:
each sleeps 4
Note: Fog signal is still operational
and may sound without warning.

Contact:
Rural Retreats,
Draycott Business Park, Draycott,
Moreton-in-Marsh, Glos GL56 9JY
Tel: 01386 701177
Email: info@ruralretreats.co.uk
www.ruralretreats.co.uk

The stormy headland at Trevose is 2½ miles in length. Fine sandy beaches adjoin the headland like bookends, but Trevose Head itself is rugged and severe, carved out of hard volcanic rock. The area is popular with surfers, who delight in the strong winds and waves along the whole Atlantic coast of Cornwall. A light for this coast was first proposed in 1809, as there were no major lights at that time on either the north Cornish or Devon coasts.

However, it took until 1st December 1847 before a light was finally established at Trevose Head, comprising Argand oil lamps backed with reflectors. Built by Thomas and Jacob Olver of Falmouth, the tower was situated on the north west extremity of the headland, with gigantic cliffs of grey granite rising sheer from the sea to a height of 150ft or more. The area, like so much of the Devon and Cornish coastline is constantly threatened by sea mists that make even the most powerful lights seem like candles. Despite being regularly shrouded in sea mist, a fog signal was not initially installed.

Originally there were two fixed lights at Trevose Head, the High Light in the tower that still stands, and a separate Low Light housed in a second lantern placed at the base of the tower. In 1882 the main light was changed to an occulting character, whereby the period that the light is shown is greater than the time it is eclipsed. The Low Light was then discontinued, and the complement of two men were increased to three.

The first mention of a fog signal in the Station Order Book occurred during the time when Lord Rayleigh was scientific adviser to Trinity House. In the autumn of 1911 the dwellings underwent extensive alterations and work to construct a fog signal house began. The new fog signal went into operation on 6th February 1913, at an inauguration ceremony attended by Deputy Master Captain Blake and Captains Crawford and Marshall, accompanied by Sir Thomas Matthews.

The new fog horn, an enormous trumpet, was developed by Lord Rayleigh, who was experimenting at that time with new types of fog signal. Rectangular in shape the new horn was 36ft long with the resonator 18ft wide by 2ft high, it being intended that this shape would give a wide horizontal spread of sound. It stayed in use until a new Supertyphon signal was introduced in 1963.

Around 1912 the lighthouse was modernised, and a first order lens with three symmetrical panels was put into service. At this time the character was altered to a flashing red light. A newly developed Hood vapour burner was installed in the 1920s. This high power vapourised oil burner, with autoform mantle was a great improvement. The lighthouse had a character of a red flash every 5 seconds with a visibility of 25 miles, and a fog horn giving two blasts every 30 seconds.

Trevose Lighthouse was automated in 1995, the existing optic being retained but the rotation speed was slowed to alter the character to one flash every 7½ seconds. The red screens were removed to give a white light. The lamp was changed to a 35 watt metal halide in a two position lamp changer. The air fog signal was replaced by an electric omnidirectional signal controlled by a fog detector. The lighthouse is now monitored from the Trinity House Operations Control Centre at Harwich in Essex

The holiday cottages are located in two semi-detached dwellings either side of the lighthouse tower. There is a paved courtyard to the rear of the dwellings, with a small lawned area in front; however beyond the perimeter the cliffs fall steeply to the sea below, children should be supervised at all times.

Established:	1847
Height of tower:	27 metres
Elevation of light:	62 metres
Automated:	1995
Character:	1 white flash every 7.5 seconds
Range of light:	21 miles
Fog signal:	2 blasts every 30 seconds
Access to tower:	None

Three self-catering cottages:
two sleep 4, one sleeps 3
Note: Fog signal is still operational and may sound without warning.

Contact:
Rural Retreats,
Draycott Business Park, Draycott,
Moreton-in-Marsh, Glos GL56 9JY
Tel: 01386 701177
Email: info@ruralretreats.co.uk
www.ruralretreats.co.uk

The village of Pendeen lies on the dramatic north coast of Cornwall halfway between Lands End and St Ives. Like many other old Cornish coastal villages, Pendeen was believed to be a secret place for smuggling activities, and boasts three beaches although some are more accessible than others. The largest of the three beaches was for many years the home of a wrecked ship until the army was called in to clear the wreck as it presented a danger to swimmers. Overlooking Pendeen, above the Church, is a hill which the locals have nicknamed "Slidehill Cemetery", because of the graves at the bottom. A mile from the village stands Pendeen Lighthouse, situated on a headland known as Pendeen Watch.

Below the lighthouse can be found the wreck of *The Liberty,* although most of it has now been eroded away by the sea parts of the wreck are still visible at low tide on what locals call 'Liberty Rock' which is a favourite fishing spot.

The height of cliffs along this section of coastline prevented passing vessels from catching sight of either Trevose Head Lighthouse to the east or Longships Lighthouse to the west. As a result, many were unable to ascertain their position and came to grief on the exposed rocks near Pendeen. However it was not until the late 1800s that Trinity House decided to erect a lighthouse and fog signal here to guide shipping between Cape Cornwall to the west and Gurnards Head to the east.

The lighthouse was built in 1900 by Arthur Carkeek of Redruth, under the direction of Trinity House Engineer in Chief Sir Thomas Matthews. The tower was constructed of rubble stone with a cement facing, and stands 56ft high and 195ft above sea level. Before work could begin the cap of the Point had to be removed and the whole headland flattened. A huge retaining wall was built on the seaward side.

The light was finally lit on 26th September 1900, using a five wick Argand Lamp. This was replaced in 1926 when the light was electrified. The original optic is still in use, weighs 2½ tons, and floats on a mercury bath.

In the past a strange quirk of this lighthouse and that at Trevose further along the coast, was that the flash of each lighthouse was visible from the other, but only at low tide, as the curvature of the earth obscured the lights as the tide rose. This phenomena no longer occurs as the nominal range of the lights has been reduced. Pendeen Lighthouse has an intensity of 150,000 candle power, giving the four flashes every 15 seconds a range of 16 miles.

The lighthouse was automated in 1995 and is now monitored from the Trinity House Operations Control Centre in Essex. The very loud compressed air fog signal (as shown in the picture below) is no longer used at Pendeen, however in times of poor visibility a lesser electric signal gives one blast every 20 seconds.

The accommodation is provided in the terrace of dwellings located immediately behind the tower, there is a large lawned area in front of the cottages, with paved parking areas to the side. At the rear of each cottage is a small gravelled courtyard. Beyond the perimeter walls the cliffs fall steeply to the sea below, children should be supervised at all times.

Established:	1900
Height of tower:	17 metres
Elevation of light:	59 metres
Automated:	1995
Character:	4 white flashes every 15 seconds
Range of light:	16 miles
Fog signal:	1 blast every 20 seconds
Access to tower:	None

Six self-catering cottages:
three sleep 6, two sleep 4,
one sleeps 8
Note: Fog signal is still operational and may sound without warning.

Contact:
Cornish Cottages Ltd, Mullion Meadows, Mullion, Helston, Cornwall TR12 7HB
Tel: 01326 240333
Email: enquiries@cornishcottagesonline.com
www.cornishcottagesonline.com

The craggy outcrop of the Lizard peninsula is the most southerly headland of mainland Britain, and is a landfall and coastal mark guiding vessels traversing along the English Channel. At one time it was also a headland much frequented by smugglers and wreckers.

In the early 17th century, the Lizard was owned by Sir John Killigrew of Arwenack House, Falmouth. In partnership with his cousin, Lord Dorchester, Killigrew proposed the construction of a lighthouse to Trinity House to discourage the local people from showing false lights. Trinity House disagreed, arguing that a lighthouse would expose the coast and guide enemy vessels and pirates to a safe landing. However, Killigrew obtained a patent directly from the Lord High Admiral, the Duke of Buckingham and agreed to erect the lighthouse at his own expense. However, he could not afford to bear the cost of maintenance, and intended to fund the project by collecting voluntary contributions from passing ships. Once completed, the lighthouse was said to be of great benefit to mariners, but the ship owners offered nothing for its upkeep, and the mounting costs of maintenance were bankrupting Killigrew. Trinity House eagerly supported all complaints about its inefficiency, maintaining that an improperly kept light was worse than no light at all. In the face of more opposition from Trinity House, James I set a levy of one halfpenny per ton on all vessels passing the light. This caused such an uproar from the shipowners that the patent was withdrawn. Eventually Killigrew ran out of money, the light was extinguished, and fell into dereliction.

It was to be another 100 years before a further light was established on the Lizard. In 1745 Captain Richard Farish put forward a proposal to build four towers on the headland. Unfortunately, during his application, he died, so Thomas Fonnereau took up the challenge. Trinity House drew up a patent in

1751 and leased the rights to Fonnereau for 61 years. Two towers with coal braziers were built, and first lit in August 1752. A cottage was built between the two towers, in which an overlooker lay on a couch so that he could keep a watch on both fires. When the bellow-blowers relaxed their efforts and the fires dimmed, he would remind them of their duties by a blast from a cow horn! Two towers were built for identification purposes, so as not to confuse them with other lights on the western approaches to the Channel.

When the lease ran out in 1812, Trinity House spent £15,000 on renovating the two light towers, and the installation of new oil lamps and reflectors. The two lights were retained as, when in line, they provided an important warning of the Manacles Reef on the east side of the Lizard. An early form of electric lighting was installed in 1883. Each tower now had a fixed electric light.

In 1903 it was decided to discontinue the western tower, and the lantern was dismantled. The lighthouse was now changed to a revolving light showing one white flash every 3 seconds from the eastern tower.

Automated in 1998 the lighthouse is now monitored from the Trinity House Operations Control Centre at Harwich in Essex. Trinity House have established an informative visitor centre based in the former engine room, with tours of the eastern tower available.

The six cottages form a terrace between the two towers, each having its own rear courtyard. Although surrounded by large lawned areas, beyond the perimeter walls the cliffs fall steeply to the sea below, children should be supervised at all times. The West Cottage incorporates the disused tower as part of the accommodation.

Established:	1752
Height of tower:	19 metres
Elevation of light:	70 metres
Automated:	1998
Character:	1 white flash every 3 seconds
Range of light:	26 miles
Fog signal:	1 blast every 30 seconds
Access to tower:	Visitor centre

8	ST ANTHONY, CORNWALL

Self-catering cottage, sleeps 4
Note: Fog signal is still operational
and may sound without warning.

Contact:
Rural Retreats,
Draycott Business Park, Draycott,
Moreton-in-Marsh, Glos GL56 9JY
Tel: 01386 701177
Email: info@ruralretreats.co.uk
www.ruralretreats.co.uk

A coal beacon originally burned at St Anthony's Head to warn ships of Black Rock in the centre of the channel into Falmouth Harbour, and also of the Manacles Rocks offshore. This beacon burned for centuries until it was replaced by the present lighthouse in 1835.

Before the lighthouse was built, the local Killigrew family flew a large red flag from an elm tree to show the direction of the wind, but this was eventually taken down in 1779 to avoid its being used by invading fleets.

The lighthouse was built by the Olver Company of Falmouth, with work starting in May 1834. It was first lit in April 1835 on the headland at the eastern entrance to Falmouth harbour. As part of the works, Trinity House also decided to erect a beacon on the Black Rock. However this was not finally completed until 1864. This large delay was primarily due to the adverse weather conditions which continually hampered the contractors, and on several occasions removed their cranes.

The light was originally provided by eight Argand oil lamps placed in front of polished reflectors, which were later replaced by a paraffin vapour burner and a Chance Brothers fixed optic.

Following an inspection by the Lighthouse Commissioners in 1881, a decision was made for a fog bell to be erected at the lighthouse. This huge bell was said to be the heaviest in Cornwall, and weighed over 2 tons; it was suspended from a beam projecting from the gallery and sounded four times every minute in poor visibility. It was replaced by a nautophone fog signal in 1954 when the lighthouse was connected to the mains electricity supply. The old bell was destined for Penwerris Church, but insufficient funds were available to erect a new bell tower to house it. After several years lying in the churchyard, the bell was eventually sent to be melted down.

St Anthony's Lighthouse was automated in 1987. Today the light character is isophase (equal periods of light and darkness) every 15 seconds, with a red sector covering the Manacles Rocks. The lighthouse is monitored from the Trinity House Operations Control Centre at Harwich in Essex.

Puppeteer Jim Henson is best known for creating *The Muppets*; but in the early 1980s Henson produced another similar series called *Fraggle Rock*. This featured another collection of strange characters that lived in a subterranean colony below the Fraggle Rock Lighthouse. The only human star of this show was the late Fulton Mackay, playing the lighthouse keeper, who along with his puppet dog Sprocket, had his life plagued by Fraggles. In the opening credits for the show the fictional lighthouse was shown, although in reality it was the St Anthony light.

The accommodation, a single dwelling, is reached via a 300 metre steep tarmac path leading down to the lighthouse from the car park on the headland above. This accommodation is not suitable for the infirm or disabled guests. It is suggested that luggage with wheels be used, as there is no vehicular access to the cottage. Beyond the perimeter walls the cliffs fall to the sea below, children should be supervised at all times. On the summit of the headland is a former nineteenth century fort now in the care of the National Trust.

Established:	1835
Height of tower:	19 metres
Elevation of light:	22 metres
Automated:	1987
Character:	Isophase white/red every 15 seconds
Range of light:	White 16 miles, Red 14 miles
Fog signal:	1 blast every 30 seconds
Access to tower:	None

Photo: Rural Retreats

9	START POINT, DEVON

Two self-catering cottages,
one sleeps 5, the other sleeps 6
Note: Fog signal is still operational
and may sound without warning.

Contact:
Rural Retreats,
Draycott Business Park, Draycott,
Moreton-in-Marsh, Glos GL56 9JY
Tel: 01386 701177
Email: info@ruralretreats.co.uk
www.ruralretreats.co.uk

Located on one of the most exposed peninsulas on the English Coast, Start Point runs sharply almost a mile into the sea on the south side of Start Bay near Dartmouth. The lighthouse, which can be found at the very end of the headland, has guided vessels along the English Channel for over 150 years.

Start Point Lighthouse was designed by Trinity House Engineer James Walker in 1836. Its gothic style architecture owes much to the fashion of the time. Two white lights were originally exhibited, one revolving and one fixed to mark the hazardous Skerries Bank. A fixed red subsidiary light is still in place below the main light.

The optic used was the first of its kind for Trinity House, being a dioptric apparatus designed by Northern Lighthouse Board Engineer Alan Stevenson, who is best remembered for the design and construction of the Skerryvore Lighthouse. Even so, the light was found to be inadequate in fog, and a bell was installed in 1865. The machinery was housed in a small building on the cliff face and operated by a weight which fell in a tube running down the sheer cliff. After only fifteen years it was replaced by a siren.

Initially the keepers at Start Point lived in the lighthouse tower; but in 1844 a three storey dwelling was built on the north side of the tower, this was followed by a similar dwelling on the south of the tower in 1873 (these were both replaced in 1957). A third dwelling, of a more grandiose design, was built in 1882 for the Principal Keeper and his family.

Since its establishment in 1836 there have been a number of casualties off the coast, many of which have run aground on the notorious Skerries reef. In 1866 the *Spirit of the Ocean* was wrecked off the reef and two years later the *Gossamer* met the same fate. The worst night of all was that of 9th March 1891 when five ships were wrecked off the Skerries, two of which, the *Morana* and the *Dryad*, went down losing all on board.

In the 1980s cracks began to appear in the ground below the fog signal house. After a new electric signal was established the old engine room was abandoned. The reverberations of the fog horn over a 60 year period are believed to have contributed to the weakening of the cliff strata. It eventually collapsed in 1990; and to further protect the lighthouse tower, the south dwelling was demolished in 1998.

Work began on the automation of Start Point Lighthouse in August 1992; this was carried out by LEC Marine at a cost of £82,754 and was completed in early 1993. The station is now monitored and controlled from the Trinity House Operations Control Centre at Harwich in Essex via a telemetry link.

Start Point is located four miles from the main road via narrow country lanes. The final stretch is a half mile private, walled, tarmac drive which runs along the side of the headland. The drive is bisected by the South West Coast Path, and walkers can detour along the drive to view the lighthouse. Start Point Lighthouse is regularly open to the public during the summer months.

Accommodation is in two cottages, Beacon Cottage (on the left in the picture above) was built in 1882; Landward Cottage (adjoining the tower) was built in 1957. There is a small courtyard between the cottages and the lighthouse tower, but it should be noted that there is no garden, and the cliffs outside of the perimeter walls fall steeply to the sea below, children should be supervised at all times.

Established:	1836
Height of tower:	28 metres
Elevation of light:	62 metres
Automated:	1993
Character:	3 white flashes every 10 seconds
Range of light:	25 miles
Fog signal:	1 blast every 60 seconds
Access to tower:	Visitor centre

PORTLAND OLD HIGH LIGHT
PORTLAND OLD LOW LIGHT, DORSET

Photo: Fran Lockyer

Portland Old Higher Light (left):
  Detached self-catering cottage, sleeps 4

Contact:
Fran Lockyer, Old Higher Lighthouse,
Portland Bill, Dorset DT5 2JT
Tel: 01305 822300
Email: enquiries@oldhigherlighthouse.com
www.oldhigherlighthouse.co.uk

Portland Old Lower Light (right):
  Self-catering: 2 or 4 bunk bed rooms,
  Self-contained cottage, sleeps 6

Contact:
Old Lower Lighthouse, Portland Bill,
Dorset DT5 2JT
Tel: 01305 820553
Email: obs@btinternet.com
www.portlandbirdobs.org.uk

The Isle of Portland is connected to the mainland by Chesil Beach, a 18 mile long spit of shingle which, at its eastern end, forms an isthmus that connects the Isle of Portland to the mainland. The southern tip of the island is known as Portland Bill, the coast here is constantly being shaped by the tides; to the south-east is the Shambles sandbank, and tidal streams of up to 7 knots have been recorded as the Portland Race rounds the Bill.

From the car park at the Bill a coastal path leads along the cliff tops to the western side of the island. It is here that the Old Higher Light can be found. There are 3 lighthouses in total at Portland; the Old Higher on the west, the Old Lower on the east, and the current Portland Bill Lighthouse at the tip. The two old lights are often confused, since the Old Higher Light is shorter than the Old Lower Light.

The first application for a lighthouse was made in 1668 by Sir John Clayton, but this fell through. Over the years many more applications were made, but were repeatedly rejected by Trinity House, the main reason, apart from expense, was that they feared the light would assist enemy ships during wartime.

A patent was finally obtained by Trinity House in 1716 and leased for a period of 61 years to a private consortium. Two lighthouses were constructed with enclosed lanterns and coal fires, but an inspection in 1752 by Trinity House officials found them to be badly maintained, and in some cases the lights had not been seen until several hours after sunset. Though improvements were made following the visit, complaints were still received from ship owners for many years afterwards. Upon expiry in 1777 the lease was returned to Trinity House, who took over maintenance of the lights.

In 1788 Samuel Wyatt, Consultant Engineer to Trinity House, supervised a rebuilding programme at the High Light. The existing coal fired lantern was removed, and Portland High light became the first lighthouse in England to be installed with Argand oil lamps; two rows of seven, containing a circular cotton wick. Highly polished square reflectors were used in conjunction with the lamps.

In 1789 a local builder, William Johns, was contracted by Trinity House to erect a new tower designed by Samuel Wyatt when the Low Light was demolished. The new 62ft high building was constructed further to the east of the tower it replaced and housed six glass reflectors.

Thomas Rogers, a glass cutter by trade, submitted a lens after requests from Trinity House during experimentation at their depot in Blackwall. His apparatus was sent to Portland, where tests continued. Rogers installed silvered glass reflectors and large plano convex lenses intended to bend the light rays to a horizontal plane. These were glazed into the lantern, and it became the first lighthouse in the world to use magnifying optical lenses. The lenses were made of solid glass, 21 inches in diameter and 5 inches thick at the focus. However the lens was soon deemed to be inefficient, the thickness of the glass was actually having a negative effect, and the lenses were removed

In 1836 a new optical apparatus was installed into the High Light, making it significantly more powerful; this was supervised by the new Consultant Engineer to Trinity House, James Walker. The Low Light was modernised again in 1856, when the dwellings were demolished and new quarters built for the keepers. Both Low and High lights were fitted with new optics and more efficient oil lamps. The High Light was also raised by 15ft to increase its range.

Trinity House decided to rebuild both towers in 1866. These were designed by James Douglass, on the recommendations of James Walker. The High Light was built as a two storey building 34ft in height. A first order dioptric lens was installed along with a Wilkins

five wicked oil lamp, and a clockwork mechanism to produce the flashes. It was first lit in March 1867, and displayed a fixed white light.

The Low Light was rebuilt to five storeys, at a height of approx 75ft, and this was lit in October 1867, displaying a fixed white light at an elevation of 210ft, visible for 21 miles. Both lights were manned by three keepers and their families. However, in 1901 fifteen ships were wrecked, and it was decided that the two lights, 1,509ft apart, were no longer suitable.

Both the Old Higher and Old Lower lights were discontinued when they were replaced by the present Portland Bill Lighthouse in 1906. The two redundant lights were auctioned in 1907, but there was little interest, and as a result the Low Light was withdrawn. The High Light was purchased for £405, and was known as Branscombe Lodge, housing its own stables. The Lower Light, or Bay View as it became known, was later converted to a bird observatory.

The Old Higher lighthouse has had many famous connections over the years. It was visited by King George III and H G Wells. More recently, the lighthouse was once owned as a holiday home by the birth control pioneer, Marie Stopes. It was derelict when purchased by the current owner in 1980. The single storey buildings alongside the tower now form part of the accommodation, and guests have access to the tower and lantern of the old lighthouse.

The observatory at the Low Light offers hostel-style accommodation, and an adjoining self-contained cottage is suitable for a family or group that requires a little more privacy. In the hostel, guests have the use of a shared kitchen, bathrooms and other facilities. In both the lighthouse and cottage, blankets and pillows are provided, but guests should bring their own linen or sleeping bags.

The current Portland Bill Lighthouse (right) was automated on 18th March 1996, and a visitor centre is now open.

Established: 1716
Present towers: 1866
Height of towers: High Light 15m,
                    Low Light 25m
Discontinued: 1906
Access to towers: Available to guests

Two self-catering cottages,
one sleeps 5, the other sleeps 6

Contact:
Rural Retreats,
Draycott Business Park, Draycott,
Moreton-in-Marsh, Glos GL56 9JY
Tel: 01386 701177
Email: info@ruralretreats.co.uk
www.ruralretreats.co.uk

One of the earliest buildings traditionally associated with the sea is the 12th century chapel of St Aldhelm's, on the headland of the same name, four miles west of Anvil Point. The building, 32ft square, with a vaulted interior carried on a central pillar, is continued through the roof in the form of a circular drum, now surmounted by a stone cross. There is no evidence of access to the drum on the roof. The most likely explanation of the tradition that a light was displayed from it is that there was originally some sort of pillar or obelisk similar to the present finial which would give the building a very distinctive silhouette from the sea in daylight, and that had a light been shown, this lofty headland would have been marked by a simple fire.

The lighthouse at Anvil Point is reached by a narrow service road and lies about a mile south west of Swanage. The area is a paradise for picnickers, and the Tilly Whim Caves, said to have been used by smugglers, are just below the lighthouse, but unfortunately for safety reasons, are no longer open to the public.

The lighthouse, which is built of local stone, was designed by Trinity House Engineer James Douglass and completed in 1881. It was officially opened by the Minister of Transport.

The short round tower is 40ft high. Its short height avoided the light being frequently shrouded in low clouds which form over this part of the

Photo: Gordon Wells

headland. The tower, dwellings and out buildings were all painted white so that during the day the lighthouse could be distinguished from the green cliffs behind it. The arc of the light is such that to the west it gives a clear line from Portland Bill and to the east guides vessels away from the Christchurch Ledge, which leads them

neatly into the Solent. The tower was originally illuminated by an incandescent paraffin vapour burner.

In 1960 the station was extensively modernised and converted from oil to mains electricity. The large original lens was removed and donated to the Science Museum in London, and replaced by a smaller optic.

It was modernised again in 1981 when the old fog signal was replaced and automatic equipment installed. The fog signal has since been discontinued. Shortly afterwards the station was downgraded to keeper and wife status. Anvil Point Lighthouse was fully automated on 31st May, 1991.

The cottages are situated in a block behind the lighthouse tower. The large grounds of the lighthouse are fully enclosed, but beyond the perimeter walls the cliffs fall steeply to the sea below, children should be supervised at all times.

Established:	1881
Height of tower:	12 metres
Elevation of light:	45 metres
Automated:	1991
Character:	1 white flash every 10 seconds
Range of light:	19 miles
Fog signal:	None
Access to tower:	Visitor centre

| 13 | **ST CATHERINE'S, ISLE OF WIGHT** |

Three self-catering cottages:
one sleeps 4, two sleep 5

Contact:
Rural Retreats,
Draycott Business Park, Draycott,
Moreton-in-Marsh, Glos GL56 9JY
Tel: 01386 701177
Email: info@ruralretreats.co.uk
www.ruralretreats.co.uk

The first light established at St Catherine's, on the southern tip of the Isle of Wight, dates back to 1323. Walter de Godyton erected a chapel and added an endowment for a priest to say masses for his family and to exhibit lights at night to warn ships from this dangerous part of the coast, both purposes being fulfilled until about 1530 when the Reformation swept away the endowment.

The present lighthouse was constructed in 1838 after the loss of the sailing ship *Clarendon*. Built of ashlar stone the lighthouse was carried up from a base plinth as a 3 tier octagon, diminishing by stages. The elevation of the light proved to be too high, as the lantern was frequently shrouded in mist, and in 1875 it was decided to lower the light by 43ft, taking about 20ft out of the uppermost section of the tower with the remainder coming out of the middle tier.

At that time the fog signal house was situated near the edge of the cliff but owing to erosion and cliff settlement the building developed such serious cracks that in 1932 a new place for the fog signal had to be found, and it was eventually mounted on a lower tower annexed to the front of the lighthouse, and built in a similar style. The resultant effect has been to give a well proportioned step down between the two towers which are now known locally as "The Cow and the Calf". The fog signal was discontinued in 1987.

The white octagonal tower has 94 steps leading up to the lantern. The main light, visible for up to 30 miles in clear weather gives a guide to shipping in the Channel as well as for vessels approaching the Solent.

A fixed red subsidiary light displayed from a window 23ft below the main light shows over the Atherfield Ledge. It is visible for 17 miles in clear weather, and was first exhibited in 1904. Both lights are electric, and standby battery lights are provided in case of a power failure.

During the Second World War, a tragic incident took place at the station. On the 1st June 1943 a bombing raid destroyed the engine house killing the three keepers on duty who had taken shelter in the building. Richard T Grenfell, Charles Tomkins and William E Jones were buried in the local cemetery at nearby Niton village, and a plaque in remembrance of them is displayed on the ground floor of the main tower.

St Catherine's Lighthouse was automated on 30th July 1997.   Prior to automation, the lighthouse had been a weather reporting station for the Meteorological Office for many years. The keepers made hourly observations including temperature, humidity, cloud height and formation, and wind direction and force. This data was then relayed to the Met Office at regular intervals. Following the de-manning of the lighthouse an automatic weather reporting station was installed which sends details of the weather conditions to the Met Office.

Accommodation is provided in the three former keepers' cottages across the courtyard from the lighthouse. Each cottage has a private enclosed courtyard and parking area. The lighthouse and grounds are enclosed by walls, but children should be supervised at all times.

The lighthouse is open at certain times, or by prior arrangement with Trinity House.

Established: 1840
Height of tower: 26 metres
Elevation of light: 41 metres
Automated: 1997
Character: 1 white flash
                       every 5 seconds
Range of light: 25 miles
Fog signal: None
Access to tower: Visitor centre

Self-catering cottage, sleeps 5
Note: Fog signal is still operational and may sound without warning.

Contact:
Rural Retreats,
Draycott Business Park, Draycott,
Moreton-in-Marsh, Glos GL56 9JY
Tel: 01386 701177
Email: info@ruralretreats.co.uk
www.ruralretreats.co.uk

A lighthouse was much needed at the eastern end of Alderney to protect shipping from the dangerous currents of the Swinge and Alderney Race, which meet close to the Island's north eastern shoreline. Numerous vessels have come to grief here, including the steamer *Behira* which foundered and later sank in 1895. Ten years later the *Portsea* sank, having been taken by the currents on to a nearby reef. Alderney's most famous wreck, the *Liverpool*, went ashore on the Island's north coast, near Fort Hommeaux Florains in February 1902. Her 6,000 tons of cargo included cement, girders, coke, marble, food stuffs, silk, soap and candles. Some of the marble found its way to Guernsey and other salvaged material was taken there by the small steamer *Pioneer*, owned by a syndicate who bought the wreck for £250. For some time the proud *Liverpool*, with sails still set on her four lofty masts, became one of the wonders of Alderney. There were trips from Guernsey to view the *Liverpool*, and attempts made to save her.

In September 1910, Trinity House invited tenders for the construction of a lighthouse. The Corporation finally accepted a tender submitted by William Baron, a resident of Alderney. In 1911 a strip of land on the island's north east coast, formerly used for drying seaweed, was handed over Trinity House. The former coast road was also deviated behind the lighthouse property for access.

In 1912 Trinity House began construction and later in the year the lighthouse was complete. The round tower, 105ft high, with a single black band, stands in the centre of its buildings, being connected to the engine room and dwellings by passages. The whole exterior is surrounded by lawns and a boundary wall.

Former lighthouse keeper WJ Lewis recounted: "One of the most spectacular sights I ever saw in Alderney was on the morning of June 3rd 1936, at 00.30

hours, when the giant zeppelin, *Hindenburg* passed on her homeward journey from South America. It was a moonlit night and the visibility was exceptionally good. The first warning of anything astir was a slight drone of engines in the distance which quickly grew into a terrific roar. I was standing with the tower blotting out my view to the west, so my first glimpse was of a brilliant light passing in line with the lantern. The *Hindenburg* quickly took shape. It was little more than a hundred feet off the ground. The light from the lighthouse lit up the underparts of the airship, so close it was. The airship's searchlight which was on the underside passed along the seaward wall of the lighthouse. The massive Swastikas were clearly seen on the steering fins aft and there was a compartment forward well lit up. As it reached the tower, the zeppelin turned and for a moment I thought her stern would strike the lantern, but she went clear and faded into the night in a north easterly direction, her searchlight playing on the waters."

With the threat of occupation in the Channel Islands from Nazi Germany a very real prospect, Alderney Lighthouse was closed down on the afternoon of 21st June 1940. The three keepers and many locals were evacuated from the island by the Trinity House tender *Vestal*. Following the liberation of the islands in 1945, Trinity House sent out inspectors from the East Cowes Depot to check for mines and booby traps, as well as reporting any repairs needed before the lighthouse could be re-lit. Alderney Lighthouse was found to be in reasonably good condition.

On 11th February 1985 a German cargo ship, *Corinna* hit the rocks near to the lighthouse. Returning to the lighthouse by air from his shore leave, keeper John Dodd flew over the Brimtides Reef, giving a good view of the stricken vessel. Seeing her from the air was the first he knew of the wreck, which could very clearly be seen from the lighthouse, only 800 yards away.

The accommodation is all located on the ground floor and there is an enclosed garden, although young children should be supervised at all times.

Photo: Rural Retreats

Established: 1912
Height of tower: 32 metres
Elevation of light: 37 metres
Automated: 1997
Character: 4 white flashes
                     every 15
                     seconds
Range of light: 23 miles
Fog signal: 1 blast
                     every 30 seconds
Access to tower: Visitor centre

Self-catering cottage, sleeps 4

Contact:
National Trust Holiday Cottages,
PO Box 536, Melksham,
Wiltshire SN12 8SX
Tel: 0844 800 2070
Email: cottages@nationaltrust.org.uk
www.nationaltrustcottages.co.uk

The famous white cliffs of Dover tower 328ft above sea level at South Foreland. Out in the English Channel great stretches of treacherous sand banks lie in wait for vessels making their crossing. One of the most notorious of these is the Goodwin Sands, known as The Great Ship Swallower, which stretches 10 miles long and three miles wide. During 1836 up to thirty vessels were lost on these sands amidst a huge storm.

The earliest record of a light at South Foreland dates from 1367 when a hermit, Nicholas de Leg, kept a light burning in a cave below the cliffs. The first record of a request for a permanent lighthouse was in 1634 when the Charles I finally granted a Scotsman, Sir John Meldrum, permission to erect two lighthouses at South Foreland with a lease for 50 years at £20 per year. The two lights originally had open fires, though by 1719 the lanterns were enclosed. However, the fires burning within the lanterns became obscured due to soot and condensation, and by 1730, under mounting pressure from ship owners, the lanterns were removed. They were not reinstated for over sixty years. In 1793 they were reinstated within a new three storey tower housing up to fourteen reflectors, with oil lamps using sperm oil. It was converted to oil gas in 1823.

In 1832 the government authorised the purchase of North and South Foreland lighthouses. In 1843 the higher lighthouse was rebuilt by Trinity House's Chief Engineer James Walker. This is the 69ft high tower which stands today, with its castellated parapet and dwellings adjoining the building. The lower light, an octagonal white tower 49ft in height, very similar in design to that of the higher light, was rebuilt three years later in 1846. The cost of these modifications including new lamps and lens was estimated at £4,409. In 1869 further land was acquired between the two lights for engine houses, workshops and living accommodation for the three keepers.

Between 1856 and 1885 a number of lighting experiments were carried out, and in December 1858 a magneto-electric light was tested at the lighthouse by Professor Holmes. It was the strongest artificial light known at that time. In 1872, the higher lighthouse was the first to be lit with a permanent electricity source, producing 150,000 candlepower. However, Professor Holmes' machine was short-lived, as a new dynamo-electric system was tested in 1876-7 by Dr Siemens, which proved a far superior illumination to the magneto-electric machine.

Other experiments were carried out at the lighthouse between 1884 and 1885, testing out gas illumination in preference to electricity. Three temporary lights were established on the headland to record these tests. Further experiments were also carried out with fog signals.

1898 marked another milestone in South Foreland's history, when the Italian Guglielmo Marconi made his first ship to shore radio broadcast on 24th December from the lighthouse to the East Goodwin Lightvessel, 10 miles away. The following spring the lightship was the first vessel to send its own distress signal, and was able to summon help when it was run down by the *RF Matthews* .

In 1903 two fixed electric lights shone from the towers, which had originally been designed as leading lights to be lined up from the south end of the Goodwins. However, due to the constant shifting of the Goodwin Sands the lower light was discontinued in 1904.

The lighthouse was automated in 1959, and the tower was modernised in 1969 when it was finally connected to the national grid, with a standby generator. It was discontinued on 30th September 1988, and acquired by the National Trust in the following year.

Accommodation is in the East Cottage. Access is down a long unadopted private road which is very uneven and rough in places. The lawned area in front of the cottage is fenced off, but beyond this wall, the cliffs fall away steeply, young children should be supervised at all times.

Established:	1634
Present tower	1843
Height of tower:	21 metres
Discontinued:	1988
Access to tower:	Visitor centre

Two self-catering cottages, each sleeps 4

Contact:
Rural Retreats,
Draycott Business Park, Draycott,
Moreton-in-Marsh, Glos GL56 9JY
Tel: 01386 701177
Email: info@ruralretreats.co.uk
www.ruralretreats.co.uk

A light was first exhibited on the North Foreland in 1499. This was a swape light, which consisted of a long pivoted beam, heavy at its short end, and tapering to the long end from which, suspended on a length of chain, was a basket containing an open fire. This light was often difficult to see, sometimes hampered by its own smoke.

The first real lighthouse built on the Foreland was erected in 1636. It was built by John Meldrum, one of the great entrepreneurs of lighthouse ownership. The two storey octagonal tower was made of timber, lath and plaster, but in 1683 it caught fire and burnt down.

A new lighthouse, 34ft tall, made of brick, stone and flint was built in 1691. It carried a fire basket and exhibited a fixed white light.

The lighthouses of North and South Foreland were owned as an investment by the directors of Greenwich Hospital, although some of the money raised by the lights went towards their upkeep.

In 1793 the octagonal tower was heightened by adding two more storeys, and the coal fired beacon was replaced by eighteen Argand oil lamps, with circular wicks.

Trinity House purchased North and South Foreland Lighthouses in 1832, the Admiralty transferring them directly from Greenwich Hospital. In 1872 electric power was introduced to the North and South Forelands on the instruction of Michael Faraday, then Scientific Adviser to Trinity House. These became the first lighthouses in the world to be electrically powered.

The lighthouse was further heightened in 1890 when the lantern was built on the top of the tower to house the light itself. It now stood 85ft high.

Although the sites of the lighthouse out buildings have changed, the site of the tower has not changed. Since the alterations in 1890 the tower has been painted white.

In 1930 North Foreland was fully electrified with electric filament lamps being installed, giving a light range of 21 miles. Its present character is 5 white or red flashes every 20 seconds.

Today North Foreland stands sentinel on top of a chalk headland to warn ships off the treacherous Goodwin Sands seven miles off the coast to the east, and the less infamous Margate Sands to the North. For navigators, it also marks the junction of the Dover Strait and the Thames Estuary.

In November 1998 North Foreland was the last lighthouse in the British Isles to be automated in a ceremony attended by the Deputy Master of Trinity House, HRH Duke of Edinburgh.

The two cottages are situated either side of the tower. Originally they would have had direct access to the tower, but this has since been sealed. Both two storey cottages have shared use of a large lawned garden.

Established:	1636
Present tower:	1793
Height of tower:	26 metres
Elevation of light:	57 metres
Automated:	1998
Character:	5 white/red flashes every 20 seconds
Range of light:	White 19 miles, Red 16 miles
Fog signal:	None
Access to tower:	None

Hostel accommodation, 36 berths

Contact:
Fellowship Afloat Charitable Trust,
The Sail Lofts, Woodrolfe Road,
Tollesbury, Essex CM9 8SE
Tel: 01621 868113
Email: info@fact.org.uk
www.fact.org.uk

Trinity lies in a salt marsh berth at Tollesbury, in the well known Blackwater Estuary. She has modern accommodation for 36 guests; groups from schools and youth clubs are the main stay. The RYA dinghy and powerboat programme also serves adults. During winter months watercolour painting, bird watching and retreat weekends feature.

Built in 1954 for Trinity House by shipbuilders Philip and Son of Dartmouth, she was launched on 18th November 1952, and first saw service on the Morecambe Bay station in February 1954. She was stationed at numerous positions, the last one being Dudgeon in June 1984. On 21st March 1987 she was moved to Harwich, and in the following year tenders for purchase were received.

Fellowship Afloat approached Trinity House, and the tender was accepted. She was towed to Tollesbury on 30th September 1988, and officially dedicated on 27th May 1991, shortly afterwards she was renamed *Trinity*.

Today *Trinity* is moored in Woodrolfe Creek, a sheltered inlet on the north side of the River Blackwater. The Fellowship Afloat Charitable Trust (FACT) converted her to a residential centre in 1990. It was carried out ensuring that her exterior appearance was little changed. Inside all work has been carried out in keeping with its original character.

Length: 42 metres
Constructed: 1954
Discontinued: 1987

Self-catering cottage, sleeps 4-5

Contact:
English Country Cottages
Stoney Bank, Earby, Barnoldswick,
BB94 0AA
Tel: 0870 238 9922
www.english-country-cottages.co.uk

The need for a lighthouse between Cromer and Winterton was brought home by a terrible storm in 1789, which saw the loss of over 70 ships and 600 sailors off the Norfolk coast. Originally two lighthouses were built, the present tower and another lower lighthouse on the cliff edge. By keeping the lights in line, one above the other, vessels were guided clear of the southern end of the notorious Haisborough Sands. The two lighthouses were lit for the first time on the evening of January 1st 1791.

In 1865 Cannel gas was introduced on an experimental basis in place of the original Argand oil lamps. As the lighthouse was not sufficiently close to any mains gas supply, the gas was manufactured within the grounds of the high light. It was produced in five coal-fired retorts, and stored in two small gas holders standing nearby. An incandescent vapour burner replaced the coal gas in 1904, and this itself was replaced in 1929 by Acetylene, which made it possible to dispense with the need for resident keepers. Originally, there had been four lighthouse keepers and their families at Happisburgh (two at each lighthouse).

Photo: Gill Cullingford

The helically framed lantern was erected in 1863 to replace an earlier wooden lantern house. It consists of diagonal frames that cross each other at a constant angle, and thus there are no blind spots behind the lantern framework. When the prismatic optic was installed in 1868, Happisburgh exhibited a fixed light. However in 1883, just prior to the closure of the cliff top low light, the light character was changed to occulting - the light was exhibited for 25 seconds, followed by a 5 second eclipse. This was achieved by having a clockwork hood that would lower and obscure the then gas lamp for 5 seconds every half minute.

Following improvements to the High Light, the cliff top Low Light was discontinued in 1883 when threatened by erosion, and demolished shortly after. The optic previously in use at the Low Light was put into storage, and later transferred to the newly built lighthouse at Southwold in Suffolk, in 1889. Now there was only one tower at Happisburgh, it became necessary to differentiate the white beacon during daylight hours, and so the red bands were added.

Although most lighthouses produce a flash character by rotating an optic with an annular lens around a fixed light source, here the optic is fixed, and it is the lamp itself that flashes on and off.

With the switch to Acetylene in 1929, Happisburgh became an "unwatched" lighthouse, though a local attendant was on hand should anything go wrong. The two adjoining cottages were then sold, and became private dwellings. The Acetylene became the standby light source once electricity was installed in 1947, and at the same time, the light character was altered to 3 flashes every 30 seconds - the lighthouse still retains this character today.

In 1988 the lighthouse was due to be decommissioned by Trinity House, who were carrying out a review of navigation aids around the coast. The Friends of Happisburgh Lighthouse were formed to lobby for retention of the light. Two years later, following an Act of Parliament, the Happisburgh Lighthouse Trust was established to assume responsibility for the maintenance and operation of the light. In July 1990 to mark the handover, Her Royal Highness the Queen Mother visited the lighthouse, and the following month the lighthouse featured in the BBC Programme *Challenge Anneka*, during which it was repainted, and a new lighting and back up battery system was installed.

As well as being East Anglia's oldest working lighthouse, it is also the UK's only independently run operational lighthouse. The lighthouse is open to visitors on weekends during the summer.

The cottage has two bedrooms, one double, one twin. The cottage has its own garden, which is enclosed by its own wall.

Established:	1791
Height of tower:	26 metres
Elevation of light :	41 metres
Automated:	1929
Character:	3 white flashes every 30 seconds
Range of light:	14 miles
Fog signal:	None
Access to tower:	Visitor Centre

Two self-catering cottages,
one sleeps 6, the other sleeps 2

Contact:
Rural Retreats,
Draycott Business Park, Draycott,
Moreton-in-Marsh, Glos GL56 9JY
Tel: 01386 701177
Email: info@ruralretreats.co.uk
www.ruralretreats.co.uk

Before a lighthouse was established at Cromer, lights were shown from the tower of the parish church. Although small, these served a useful purpose for many years.

Following Charles II's restoration in 1660 many proposals were put forward to establish lighthouses on all parts of the coast. Sir John Clayton, one of the proposers, suggested no less than five lighthouses on four different sites - at the Farne Islands off Northumberland, Flamborough Head in Yorkshire, two at Corton near Lowestoft, and one at Foulness, Cromer.

Despite opposition to his schemes Clayton, together with George Blake, obtained a comprehensive patent in 1669 and at a cost of £3,000 erected towers at each of the four sites. The patent would last for 60 years and specified rates of voluntary dues to be paid by the owners of passing vessels.

Unfortunately the cost of maintenance was high and many of the ship owners were unwilling to pay the dues required so that Clayton could not afford to kindle fires in the tower at Cromer. However the unlit tower served as a beacon and together with the other towers were marked definitely as lighthouses on sea charts after 1680 with references such as "a lighthouse but no fire kept in it".

The owner of the land at Foulness, Nathaniel Life, considered that the situation required a lighthouse, and it is said that he built a tower in 1717 hoping to be granted a patent for the light. It is more likely, however, that Life merely took steps for lighting the shell of Clayton's tower. Assisted by Edward Bowell, a Younger Brother of Trinity House, he persuaded the Brethren to apply for a patent, which they obtained in 1719, the dues to be ¼ penny per ton of general cargo and ½ penny per chaldron (25 cwt) of Newcastle coal. Life and Bowell jointly received a lease at a rental of £100, on Life's undertaking that the tower and grounds should pass to Trinity House when the patent expired in 61 years. The patentees exhibited a coal fire which was enclosed in a lantern on 29th

September 1719.

In 1792 Trinity House, now in possession of the lighthouse, installed only the second flashing light apparatus in the Service; 5 reflectors and Argand oil lamps on each of the 3 faces of a revolving frame. The frequent and rapid eclipse of the light annoyed some mariners, who described it as an "ignis fatus" or "will'-o-the-wisp".

It is reputed that the first keepers were two young women who together received a pound a week for wages with certain prerequisites. However, the sea encroached rapidly, with large cliff falls in 1799 and 1825. A new lighthouse was built in 1833, and Bowell's tower was finally destroyed by a landslip in 1866.

The new lighthouse, standing well back from the cliff edge, was a 60ft octagonal tower. The lighthouse was converted to electric operation in 1958, and in June 1990 the station was switched to automatic operation and is now monitored from the Trinity House Operations Control Centre at Harwich. The Royal Cromer Golf Course is located adjacent to the grounds.

One of the former keepers' cottages provides holiday accommodation, the other unit is a small studio apartment alongside the tower. The latter has its bedroom in the basement of the lighthouse itself. Both cottages have a wall surrounding the courtyard, and the area between the tower and the cliff edge is a picturesque

parkland area known as Happy Valley.

Established: 1719
Present tower: 1833
Height of tower: 18 metres
Elevation of light: 84 metres
Automated: 1990
Character: 1 white flash
                       every 5 seconds
Range of light: 21 miles
Fog signal: None
Access to tower: None

Self-catering cottage, sleeps 8

Contact:
Norfolk Country Cottages,
Carlton House, Market Place,
Reepham, Norfolk NR10 4JJ
Tel: 01603 871872
Email: info@norfolkcottages.co.uk
www.norfolkcottages.co.uk

Around 1272 a chapel was built on the cliffs overlooking St Edmund's Point. It quickly became an established seamark effectively pinpointing the entrance to The Wash. After many years the old chapel fell into decay and was superseded by a conventional lighthouse, which became known to sailors as "The Chapel Light".

In 1663 a syndicate of Lynn merchants proposed a lighthouse to indicate the entrance to The Wash, and by 3rd June 1665 a pair of lighthouse towers had been established beside the old chapel on Hunstanton cliff, first lit in October 1665, originally from a coal fired light and a front light illuminated by candles. The two lights formed a pair of leading lights which would guide ships safely through a passage between Sunk Sand and the Stubborn Sand.

Between 1711 and 1750 the front light was discontinued, due to changes in the coastline. In 1777 a devastating fire occurred, and the tower was completely destroyed and had to be rebuilt. This new tower stood upon Hunstanton cliff, and was built of timber. Lit for the first time in 1778, its new light was brilliant. Ezekiel Walker installed a number of reflectors with an oil lamp.

On 21st February 1828 a lightvessel, *Lynn Well*, at the head of the Long Sand, in the mouth of The Wash, brought about significant improvements to the lighting of the estuary.

By 1832 lighting improvements were made to the lighthouse, and the current leaseholder Samuel Lane was granted an extension to maintain the lighthouse and continue to collect the tolls. When he died in April 1835, ownership was transferred to his son Frederick, who sought permission from Trinity House to change the colour of the reflectors shining over the Roaring Middle Sand to red.

In August 1836 Trinity House purchased the lease and made plans to replace the timber lighthouse which had now been standing for 60 years. The new light housed a number of Argand lamps and polished reflectors. The red reflectors facing the Roaring Middle Sand was maintained, but the remaining arc of its coverage displayed a fixed white light which shone for the first time in September 1840.

In the late 19th century the lighthouse was painted with two broad red bands.

From 1872 through to 1907 a chain of floating lights rendered the presence of a light on the cliff at Hunstanton superfluous. During the War the lighthouse was used as an Admiralty Wireless Station, rumoured to be intercepting German messages and breaking their codes. Early in 1921 Trinity House announced their intention to discontinue the light, which was lit for the last time on the night of 29th September 1921.

On Thursday 5th January 1922 at Hunstanton Town Hall, the whole lighthouse property including the tower and dwellings were sold at auction for £1,300. It was purchased the by owner of the Hunstanton Estate, Mr Charles Alfred le Strange. The lantern and its lighting equipment was removed by Trinity House.

Between the two World Wars the decapitated tower stood unused, whilst the ancillary premises were used as a café and tea rooms. At the outbreak of the Second World War in 1939 the former lighthouse was commandeered by the military authorities for use as an observation post and gunnery control. This resulted in a brickwork extension above the gallery. Shortly after the War the lighthouse was acquired by Hunstanton Urban District Council who leased it, firstly as a commercial enterprise, probably tea rooms, and later as living accommodation.

In 1964 the former lighthouse was put up for sale and purchased by a private bidder. Extensive alterations were carried out, and in 1965 one of the keepers cottages was demolished, and additions were made to the remaining one. The tall chimney stacks, trade marks of Trinity House dwellings were also removed.

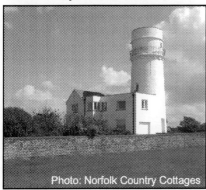
Photo: Norfolk Country Cottages

The tower does not form part of the accommodation, which comprises four bedrooms, but there is access for the views. The grounds are enclosed by a wall, but children should be supervised at all times.

Established:	1665
Present tower:	1840
Height of tower:	18 metres
Discontinued:	1921
Access to tower:	Available to guests

Bed and Breakfast accommodation

Contact:
Jim Deighton,
Paull Old Lighthouse, Paull,
Near Hull, East Yorkshire HU19 8AJ
Tel: 01482 896702 / 07894 951324
Email: jim@jamesdeighton.co.uk

It is thought that a light was first established at Paull in the mid 1500s. From 1567 onwards there are various references to the repair of a wooden beacon at Paull.

In 1820 Robert Thompson bought the land where the present lighthouse is located. The tower was established in 1836 to the design of Francis Dales, who also designed the sister lights on the other side of the Humber estuary at Killingholme. An inscription on the outside wall says that the lighthouse was built by William Collinson and George Hall, Wardens of Trinity House of Kingston-upon-Hull. When in operation the tower exhibited a fixed white light with a range of 7 miles, guiding shipping both approaching and leaving the upper reaches of the Humber.

Cottages linking the two terraces to the tower were added later, although Penny Cottages, along Town End Road were later demolished, apart from one attached to the lighthouse. Further extensions have since been added.

It is rumoured that there are tunnels running from the building to the beach, and could have been used for smuggling. However, the entrances have long been blocked up.

This single light was soon considered insufficient and was replaced by a pair of leading lights at Thorngumbald Clough in 1870. In 1985 the current owner Jim Deighton purchased the lighthouse for £45,000.

Established: 1567
Present tower: 1836
Height of tower: 13 metres
Discontinued: 1870
Access to tower: Available to guests

Photo: Trinity House

Full board accommodation,
6 double en-suite cabins
Note: With some exceptions,
cruises are available from
April to October.

Contact:
Strand Voyages,
357 Strand,
London WC2R 0HS
Tel: 020 7010 9290
Email: voyages@strandtravel.co.uk
www.strandtravel.co.uk

THV *Patricia*, the Trinity House flagship, is one of five lighthouse tenders that look after and service the maritime navigation aids around the British Isles. Work includes refuelling offshore lights, maintenance, towing, buoy work, and wreck location and marking. Built by Robb Caledon in Leith in 1982, *Patricia* is 284ft long and 2,541 gross tons.

She is fitted with towing winches providing a routine capability for moving lightvessels to and from their stations. She has a 20 tonne speed crane capable of lifting the largest navigational buoys, and there is a helideck aft.

The current *Patricia* is the third with that name, in 1994 she led the Royal Yacht *Britannia* at the D-Day 50th Anniversary Fleet Review. She is fitted with additional accommodation for the annual inspection voyages by the Trinity House Elder Brethren. When the Brethren are not aboard, this accommodation is available for the use of up to twelve passengers whilst THV *Patricia* undergoes her normal servicing duties.

Photo: Trinity House

Built: 1982
Length: 86 metres
Beam: 14 metres
Draught: 4.5 metres
Speed: 14 knots
Gross tonnage: 2541

Two self-catering cottages,
each sleeps 5

Contact:
Rural Retreats,
Draycott Business Park,
Draycott, Moreton-in-Marsh,
Glos GL56 9JY
Tel: 01386 701177
Email: info@ruralretreats.co.uk
www.ruralretreats.co.uk

It is thought that there may have been a lighted beacon close to Whitby in Roman times, for Bede in his "Ecclesiastical History of the English Nation" wrote that the Romans had built along the eastern coasts numerous towers for the protection against the incursions of Saxon and Danish pirates. He seems to have thought that these towers were to serve also as lighthouses, for he interprets Streonshalh (Whitby) to mean Sinus Fari, the Bay of the Lighthouse. Certainly there is the remains of a tower which may have once been used as a lighthouse in the village of Dunsley, a few miles north of Whitby.

Located at the mouth of the River Esk, the fishing town and former whaling centre of Whitby is the only deep water anchorage of the North Yorkshire coast. Entry into the harbour was often difficult, so two breakwaters were built each with a lighthouse at the end. The west breakwater lighthouse was built in 1835 and is open to the public in summer. The east breakwater lighthouse was built in 1855. In 1914 the two piers were extended, new beacons were established on the extremities of each, and the west pier lighthouse shone only when a vessel was expected and when entry into the harbour was safe.

In 1858 two further lighthouses were constructed on Ling Hill, approximately two miles east of Whitby harbour, to the designs of James Walker, Consultant Engineer to Trinity House. The north and south towers when aligned, would clearly mark the off lying Whitby Rock, on which many ships bound for the port foundered. The south tower (or rear light), which is still operational today, was 45ft high and the north tower (or front light), which was built on a lower section of cliff, was 66ft high. Both towers displayed fixed lights.

In 1870 the two lights on Ling Hill had a range of 23 miles. Modernisation took place in 1890 when the character of the rear light was altered from a fixed to an occulting light, and a vertical ruby strip in the lantern of the tower was installed, which shone a red sector over the dangerous Whitby Rock. The occulting light with its red sector had a 30 second character, the light being visible for 27½ seconds, then eclipsed for 2½ seconds, with a range of 22 miles. At the same time the north (front) light was discontinued, with Whitby Rock also marked by a buoy.

The fog signal building at Whitby is on the site of the former front light. It is now owned as a private residence, as the signal is no longer in use. The fog signal gave 4 blasts every 90 seconds. When operated, the powerful siren was known locally as the Hawsker Bull and could be heard up to 10 miles away.

In the early 1970s the lighthouse still had an occulting mechanism, although it was now a 15 second cycle. The optic, a first order catadioptric system, was lighted by a paraffin vapour burner, which gave the light an intensity of 57,000 candle power with a range of 22 miles.

The lighthouse was modernised in 1976 when mains electricity was installed and the light changed to an isophase character, ie equal periods of light and darkness. The ruby strip in the lantern still marks Whitby Rock along with a bell buoy positioned offshore. The intensity was increased to around 400,000 candle power with a range of 24 miles.

The two cottages are surrounded by a lawned area enclosed by stone walls, but beyond these walls the cliffs fall steeply to the sea below, children should be supervised at all times.

Established:	1858
Height of tower:	13 metres
Elevation of light:	73 metres
Automated:	1992
Character:	Isophase white/red every 10 seconds
Range of light:	White 18 miles Red 16 miles
Fog signal:	None
Access to tower:	None

Two self-catering cottages,
each sleeps 4

Contact:
National Trust Holiday Cottages,
PO Box 536, Melksham,
Wiltshire SN12 8SX
Tel: 0844 800 2070
Email: cottages@nationaltrust.org.uk
www.nationaltrustcottages.co.uk

By the mid 1800s, the shipping trade along the north east coast was expanding rapidly. In 1869 over 20 vessels had been lost in one year alone between South Shields and Sunderland. Trinity House soon realised the urgency for a light on this stretch of coastline, and Lizard Point, situated between the two ports was chosen. As there was already a lighthouse at Lizard Point in Cornwall, it was named after nearby Souter Point.

Designed by Trinity House engineer Sir James Douglass, it was completed on 11th January 1871. Seventy six steps lead up to the lantern, affording coastal views of up to 40 miles on a clear day, from Whitby to the south and northwards to Coquet Island. Originally the lighthouse was painted white, but a red band was added in September 1924 to further distinguish it as a daymark.

Prior to its installation, the apparatus and machinery were displayed at the Paris Exhibition of 1867. Souter became known as the world's first reliably electrified lighthouse, winning international acclaim for its technological advancement.

From 1871 through to 1915 a carbon arc lamp produced the light by passing an electric current between two carbon rods to create a spark. The main light flashed once every 30 seconds, with a fixed red subsidiary light which shone across the offshore obstructions of Mill Rock, White Stones and Hendon Rock. This was produced by directing stray light from the main lamp downwards through an opening in the floor to another reflector, placed to refract it through a window lower down the tower.

In 1915 the lighthouse was modernised and the lighting apparatus changed to oil, the light being visible for 18 miles. A first order biform flashing optic was installed, consisting of two optics, mounted one on top of the other, each with its own lamp. The lantern had to be extended in height to accommodate these two large optics, changing the appearance of the top of the tower. The optical apparatus, weighing 4½ tons floated on a bath of mercury to ease friction, and the unit was rotated by a weight-driven clockwork mechanism. On one occasion the weights inside the tube in the centre of the tower got stuck, so the keeper on watch had to wake his colleague for assistance. For a whole hour, he had to turn the lens by hand, while the other struggled to free the weights to set the clockwork mechanism in motion again. The clockwork mechanism was later replaced by an electric motor.

The lens arrangement for the subsidiary light was renewed in 1919, and in the same year the colour and character of the main light changed from one white flash every 30 seconds to one red flash every 5 seconds.

On 25th June 1952 the lighting reverted from mantle burners to electricity, using incandescent lamps, the main light being 3,500 watts, with a 500 watt standby lamp in reserve.

Six cottages were originally built for the keepers, one for a qualified Engineer, who was in overall charge, and four for the Assistant Keepers. In the 1881 census, it was recorded that the Engineer, Henry Millet, was living at the lighthouse with his wife, 8 children, unmarried sister, and a servant. In January 1916, three of the cottages were leased to Harton Coal Company, and by November 1936, three cottages were being let out at 10 shillings (50 pence) per week. On 3rd April 1985, in a change to staffing routines, the lighthouse was altered from land to rock status, meaning that the keepers would spend a month on station, working in rotas, followed by a month's leave.

In 1987 Trinity House announced their decision to discontinue the lighthouse, "there being a preponderence of long range lights to the north and south which adequately mark the entrance to various ports". In November 1988 the light was

turned off for the last time, and the keepers were withdrawn.

The lighthouse and cottages were purchased by the National Trust and developed into a visitor centre with a shop and café that is open most days.

Accommodation is in the former keeper and engineers cottages. Both share a walled garden, but children should be supervised at all time.

Established: 1871
Height of tower: 23 metres
Discontinued: 1988
Access to tower: Visitor Centre

Hostel accommodation, sleeps 6

Contact:
Mike Martin,
6 Stormont Street
Perth PH1 5NW
Tel: 01738 633948
Email: mwa.martin@btinternet.com
www.birdobscouncil.org.uk/
    IsleofMay/body_isleofmay.htm

Lying at the mouth of the Firth of Forth, the Isle of May is perhaps best known among naturalists for its bird observatory which was established in 1934 under the auspices of the then newly formed British Trust for Ornithology. It was the first in Scotland and only the second in the British Isles, the other being on Skokholm Island off the Pembrokeshire coast. The studies of bird migration, varied seabird breeding populations, the island's own breed of mice and the island plant communities are all added attractions for visitors, in addition to the geology, the history and the lighthouses. The island was declared a National Nature Reserve in 1956.

A lighthouse has been in existence on the Isle of May since 1635. King Charles I granted a patent to James Maxwell of Innerwick and John and Alexander Cunningham to erect a beacon on the island and to collect dues from shipping for its maintenance. The light was a crude affair and consisted of a stone structure, surmounted by an iron cresset which contained a coal fire serving as the main source of illumination. Coals were hoisted to the fire by means of a box and pulley, and three men were employed the whole year round to tend the fire, which consumed about 400 tons of coal per annum. In 1791, keeper George Anderson, with his wife and 5 children were suffocated by fumes from part burnt ashes surrounding the beacon, the only family member to survive being an infant daughter, who was found alive three days later.

The old coal beacon was finally extinguished on 31st January 1816 when a new lighthouse, church-like in appearance was built, with a tower 80ft high. This lighthouse is still operational today. The grand accommodation provided for three keepers and their families. In 1843 the light was changed from a fixed light to revolving, using oil lamps, and in 1886 it became the first lighthouse in Scotland to be electrified. Paraffin was used for the light source from 1924.

About a quarter of a mile from the operational lighthouse, and on the east side of the island, stands the tower and domestic buildings of the Low Light. A light was first exhibited from this small lighthouse in 1844 to act in conjunction with the main lighthouse as leading lights, so that navigators could avoid the treacherous North Carr Rock some seven miles north of the Island. Shortly after the Low Light was established, the *Windsor Castle,* sailing from Dundee with 200 passengers aboard struck the North Carr Rocks, fortunately with no loss of life.

When the North Carr Lightship was established in 1887 to mark the rock, the Low Light was discontinued.

The Royal National Lifeboat Institution rewarded the lighthouse keepers on the Isle of May for saving lives when the *Matagorda* was wrecked in 1872, and the German Government sent a pair of binoculars each to Robert Grierson and Laurence Anderson, who helped the crew of the *Paul*, lost on Inchkeith in 1888. In 1930 two young lighthouse keepers rescued four men by swimming off to the Aberdeen trawler *George Aunger*, which was wrecked on the North Ness, and helped them ashore.

From 1946 the former Low Light became the headquarters of the bird observatory, which had previously been situated in the Old Lookout Station.

In 1972 the lighthouse became a rock station, which meant that the keepers' families had to move to a shore station in Granton. The Isle of May Lighthouse was automated on 31st March 1989, after 353 years of manned service.

Guests staying at the Low Lighthouse must bring their own food and sleeping

bag. Priority is given to bird watchers and naturalists wishing to stay for a week, vacancies mainly arise outside peak migration periods (April-May, September–October). A boat to the island sails from Anstruther, weather permitting.

Established: 1844
Height of tower: 11 metres
Discontinued: 1887
Access to tower: None

Two self catering cottages,
one sleeps 4, the other sleeps 6

Contact:
Sheila Priest
The House, Buchan Ness Lighthouse
Boddam, Peterhead, Aberdeenshire AB42 3NF
Tel: 01779 470476
Email: info@buchannesslighthouseholidays.co.uk
www.buchannesslighthouseholidays.co.uk

The small island of Buchan Ness, located two and a half miles south of Peterhead, is linked to the village of Boddam by a short bridge.

Petitions had been made by officials in Peterhead to the Commissioners of Northern Lighthouses in 1819 to have a lighthouse erected on Buchan Ness or somewhere suitable on that part of the coast. At this time there were no significant beacons between Kinnaird Head at Fraserburgh and the Buddon Ness lighthouses at the mouth of the Tay estuary. The area was surveyed by Robert Stevenson, Engineer to the Commissioners, who decided that a light would be best sited on Buchan Ness. It was not, however, until 1827 that the light was first exhibited. John Gibb of Aberdeen was the contractor responsible for the building of the lighthouse.

Originally a fixed light had been installed at the lighthouse, but as other beacons were being established to the north and south, it became necessary to give the lights their own unique character. Kinnaird Head retained a fixed light, the 1833 Girdle Ness light at Aberdeen displayed two lights from one tower, and Buchan Ness was given a reflecting light that gave one flash every 5 seconds. This is believed to be one of the first "flashing" lighthouses in Scotland.

In 1907 the white tower was painted with a red band to better distinguish the lighthouse as a daymark from other beacons along that

coast. Further improvements were made in 1910 when the reflecting light was replaced by a dioptric lens. This involved enlarging the lantern, and as a result, its intensity was raised from 6,500 to 786,000 candlepower.

During the Second World War, on two separate occasions drifting mines were washed ashore onto nearby rocks and exploded, causing damage but fortunately no loss of life. On one occasion a mine exploded 50 yards south of the lighthouse, and three lantern panes cracked, with a further twelve glass panes broken in the tower, engine room and dwelling houses. Part of the ceilings of the kitchen and one bedroom of the First Assistant's house were brought down and the locks, hinges and bolts of four doors damaged. There were also 20 slates blown off the roof of the storehouse.

The lighthouse was converted to electric operation in 1978 and its intensity again increased, this time to 2,000,000 candlepower. At around this time a new fog signal building was erected on the corner of the complex. Now discontinued, this building still exists, whilst beyond the perimeter wall, evidence of an earlier fog siren can still be found. The lighthouse was automated in 1988 and is now remotely monitored from the Northern Lighthouse Board's headquarters in Edinburgh. John Malcolm was the last Principal Keeper, retiring from the service upon its automation.

A large walled enclosure surrounds the lighthouse and its cottages, and outside

a footpath follows the perimeter of the island. Beyond the path, the shore is very rocky and children should be supervised at all times.

Established:	1827
Height of tower:	35 metres
Elevation of light:	40 metres
Automated:	1988
Character:	1 white flash every 5 seconds
Range of light:	28 miles
Fog signal:	None
Access to tower:	None

Buchan Ness
Lighthouse Holidays

Imagine the view, smell the sea air, feel the freedom of staying in a lighthouse cottage. Now think of luxury and comfort and you're on your way to a Buchan Ness Lighthouse Holiday.

With the breathtaking scenery of one of Scotland's best kept secrets, the Buchan Coast, our lighthouse is less than an hour's drive from Aberdeen.

With miles of empty beaches, some of the best golf courses and surfing in Britain, and within easy reach of castles and whisky, our holidays offer something for everyone.

Whether you're seeking relaxation, walking, scenery, tourist attractions, history or romance, you can find it all with Buchan Ness Lighthouse Holidays.

Contact: Sheila Priest, The House, Buchan Ness Lighthouse
Boddam, Peterhead, Aberdeenshire AB42 3NF

Tel: 01779 470476
Email: info@buchannesslighthouseholidays.co.uk
www.buchannesslighthouseholidays.co.uk

61

Bed and Breakfast, Hostel accommodation and Self-catering apartment

Contact:
Rob Keeble and Val Porter,
Lighthouse Cottages, Rattray Head,
Rattray, Peterhead,
Aberdeenshire AB42 3HA
Tel: 01346 532236
Email: enquiries@rattrayhead.net
www.rattrayhead.net

Rattray Head Lighthouse was established in 1895, 46 years after Alan Stevenson, Northern Lighthouse Board Engineer, had first carried out a series of experiments to ascertain whether Rattray Briggs could be effectively marked by a red arc shown from the flashing light of Buchan Ness Lighthouse approximately 10 miles to the south. It was concluded that such a scheme was not possible.

In 1859 the Commissioners again sanctioned a series of experiments suggested by Captain Bedford, who reported that the lantern at Buchan Ness should be altered. After many experiments the Engineers reported in October 1862 and January 1863 that Rattray Briggs should be marked by the aid of a light, the position of which could only be determined after careful inspection and survey.

There was no progress until 18th November 1874, when the Sheriff of Renfrew and Bute recommended to the Northern Lighthouse Board that a lighthouse should be erected at Rattray Head. Once again the Engineer was asked to report and once again he recommended the erection of a Lighthouse on a site to be determined. Consequently, on 17th December 1874, Trinity House was requested to sanction the erection of a Lighthouse, but they refused to do so. On 18th January 1875, they wrote stating that the dangers of Rattray Briggs could be avoided by use of lead and by not coming under 20 fathoms of sounding. They suggested that a bell buoy be substituted for the one marking the reef. However, the light was finally exhibited for the first time on 14th October 1895.

Engineer David A Stevenson, nephew of Alan, built a rock tower in two parts to an unusual design, the lower containing a foghorn and engine room, and the upper the lighthouse keepers' room and lantern. It was the first time that a first class siren fog signal had been installed in a rock lighthouse.

Work began in 1892. The masonry of both portions of the tower was completed in sixteen months, spread over three seasons. The lower section, 20,000 cubic feet of dressed granite blocks, mostly quarried at Rubislaw, was 46ft high, with an entrance door reached by a 32ft outside ladder. At high water it is covered to a depth of 7ft but it is possible to walk ashore when the tide is out. The upper section, with a case diameter of 21ft for the light room, lantern and dome brings it to a total height of 120ft above the rock. The engine room is at the entrance level, and the upper tower and siren are planted on a platform known colloquially as the 'quarter deck'. The five-wick paraffin lamp, when first lit in 1895, had an intensity of 44,000 candlepower, compared to just 6,500 at neighbouring Buchan Ness.

During the Second World War, on 20th September 1941, an enemy plane circled the lighthouse and dropped three bombs, one of which did not explode. The lantern was machine-gunned but the damage caused did not seriously impair the efficiency of the apparatus. No one was injured in the attack.

Many changes have taken place since 1895. A mains electricity supply and telephone cable were laid under the seabed and completed in September 1977. In February 1982, the light was made fully automatic and the keepers withdrawn.

During the twentieth century additional accommodation was provided for the lighthouse keepers, and it is this dwelling that provides the B&B. The old granite block adjacent to this is the original shore station and contains the hostel and holiday apartment.

Established:	1895
Height of tower:	34 metres
Elevation of light:	28 metres
Automated:	1982
Character:	3 white flashes every 30 seconds
Range of light:	24 miles
Fog signal:	None
Access to tower:	None

THE MUSEUM OF SCOTTISH LIGHTHOUSES

Take a trip to Fraserburgh to visit Scotland's first lighthouse.

The Museum of Scottish Lighthouses is the only museum in Britain dedicated to telling the story of lighthouses.

In the company of our knowledgeable guides, climb the 72 steps up the castle tower to the original lighthouse. Enter the light room and take in the breathtaking views from the balcony. Then visit the lighthouse keepers cottages to learn about the demanding routine required of Kinnaird Head's first lighthouse keeper.

In the museum, discover the unique history of Kinnaird Head Lighthouse, the story of the lighthouse service in Scotland and the tale of the Stevenson family, lighthouse engineers to the world.

The museum has been nationally recognised for preserving the largest collection of lighthouse lenses and equipment in the UK.

Climbing the lighthouse can be tiring work so we have our own café overlooking the sea and gift shop for a memento of your visit.

**The museum is open seven days a week.
From April-June, Mon-Sat 10am-5pm, Sun 12am-5pm;
Jul-Aug Mon-Sat 10am-6pm, Sun 11am-6pm;
Sep & Oct Mon-Sat 10am-5pm, Sun 12am-5pm;
Nov-Mar Mon-Sat 10am-4pm, Sun 12am-4pm.
Entry is £5 for adults, £4 for students or concessions, £2 for children
(Children under 6 visit free). Group and family rates also apply.**

**For further information please phone 01346 511022,
Email info@lighthousemuseum.org.uk
or visit our website www.lighthousemuseum.org.uk**

Photo: National Trust for Scotland

Two self-catering cottages,
one sleeps 4,
the other sleeps 6

Contact:
National Trust for Scotland,
Wemyss House,
28 Charlotte Square,
Edinburgh EH2 4ET
Tel: 0131 243 9331
Email: holidays@nts.org.uk
www.ntsholidays.com

The Covesea Skerries form a group of small islands and rocks that lie off the Moray coast, 3 miles west of Lossiemouth and 1 mile west of Covesea.

It is said that a holy man, St Gerardine, who lived on the coast of Moray in the 8th or 10th century warned vessels of danger or guided them to safety past Covesea Skerries by swinging a lantern on the shore.

Many applications were made for lights to be established at Covesea Skerries and Tarbat Ness following the loss of 16 vessels during a storm in the Moray Firth in November 1826. Initially a light was placed at Tarbat Ness in preference to Covesea, but a demand for the latter was resumed in 1835.

Initially the Northern Lighthouse Board and Trinity House agreed that it was unnecessary, but letters and petitions continued; the engineer and a committee of the Board visited the coast, and eventually the Elder Brethren

Photo: Roy Thompson

were asked to look for the best site.

They recommended a lighthouse on Craighead with a beacon on Halliman's Scars, which the Commissioners agreed to. A cast iron beacon was established in 1844, and in 1846 a mainland light was shown from the Covesea Skerries Lighthouse.

Photo: Roy Thompson

The high walls that surrounded the lighthouse building for shelter caused strong whirlwinds in the courtyard and interfered with the lighthouse keepers' lookout.

In 1907 plans were made to lower these walls.

The lighthouse was automated in 1984 and is now remotely monitored from the Northern Lighthouse Board's offices in Edinburgh. The original lens can be seen in Lossiemouth Fisheries and Community Museum.

Accommodation is in the former keepers cottages, and the lighthouse complex is fenced off, though young children should be kept under supervision. There is also access to the beach via a gate from the lighthouse courtyard.

Established:	1846
Height of tower:	36 metres
Elevation of light:	49 metres
Automated:	1984
Character:	1 white/red flash every 20 seconds
Range of light:	White 24 miles Red 20 miles
Fog signal:	None
Access to tower:	None

Photo: Roy Thompson

Self-catering cottage, sleeps 6

Contact:
Mrs Anne Mackenzie,
3 Harbour Street,
Portmahomack by Tain,
Ross-shire IV20 1YG
Tel: 01862 871609
www.mackays-self-catering.co.uk

At the very tip of the long, low, windswept peninsula of Tarbat Ness stands the tall slender lighthouse of the same name with its two broad red bands, guarding the Dornoch and Moray Firths, and keeping watch over the dangerous sand bar of the Grizzen Briggs. At 134ft in height, it is the third tallest in Scotland. The location of the lighthouse is reputed to have been a site for witches gatherings, and prior to that is believed to have been a Roman fort.

Applications had been received for a lighthouse at Tarbat Ness and at Covesea Skerries near Lossiemouth as far back as 1814, as both marked the entrance to the Moray Firth which leads to the Caledonian Canal. It was not until November 1826 however, after a violent a storm had hit the Moray Firth and 16 vessels were lost in one month, that it was decided that a lighthouse at Tarbat Ness was of the utmost priority.

The lighthouse was designed by Robert Stevenson, and constructed by James Smith, a builder from Inverness. It was first lit in January 1830, using an Argand lamp with four burners displaying a white, occulting light for 2½ minutes, followed by a 30 second eclipse, visible for 18 miles. In 1892 its character was altered to six quick flashes every 30 seconds. In 1907 the lighting apparatus changed to incandescent pressurised paraffin lamps

Photo: Roy Thompson

with 55mm mantles. The machinery which was installed in 1892 and operated until its automation in 1985 is now displayed at Greenwich Maritime Museum along with its former optic. Today, its character is four white flashes every 30 seconds.

Earthquake shocks have been recorded at the lighthouse, and on one occasion shook the tower

Photo: Roy Thompson

so much that the shades and lamp glasses rattled. The lighthouse was automated in 1985, when the Principal Keeper Jack Clark left for the last time.

The two semi-detached keepers cottages are situated 15ft in front of the tower, and face out towards the north west. They were sold privately in 1986, and are listed as a category 'A' Building of Special Architectural and Historic Interest. The two cottages are set in two acres of lawn.

Outside the walls, a maritime heath in a nature conservancy area boasts sea grasses and heather. The average annual rainfall in the area is only about 24 inches, making it one of the lowest in the UK, and it is a particularly sheltered area. It is also a Special Protection Area under the European Union Wild Birds Directive, as it is a stopping off point for migratory birds in the Autumn.

The grounds are walled and fenced. The cottage providing holiday accommodation is all on one level.

Established:	1830
Height of tower:	41 metres
Elevation of light:	53 metres
Automated:	1985
Character:	4 white flashes every 30 seconds
Range of light:	24 miles
Fog signal:	None
Access to tower:	None

Photo: Christine Willers

Two self-catering cottages,
one sleeps 3,
the other sleeps 4

Contact:
Cantick Head Lighthouse,
Longhope, Orkney KW16 3PQ
Tel: 01856 701255
Email: cantick@gmail.com
www.orkneylighthouse.com

The Pentland Firth which separates the islands of Orkney from the north eastern tip of Scotland, has been known to be extremely dangerous, with some of the most treacherous eddies and currents anywhere in Britain. One of the finest natural harbours of the world can be found here at Scapa Flow, which is almost encircled by the islands. It was a vital anchorage during both World Wars. In 1914 Scapa Flow became the base for the Royal Navy's Grand Fleet, and it is where the German Fleet were interned in 1919.

The Commissioners of Northern Lighthouses made representations to Trinity House and the Board of Trade in February 1854 and received almost immediately statutory approval to their proposals. Lengthy correspondence did, however, take place with Trinity House and the Board of Trade regarding approval of specification, character of light and acceptance of building tenders which delayed commencement of building work until February 1856.

Marking the southern entrance on the south east coast of the island of Hoy, Cantick Head Lighthouse was first exhibited on the night of 15th July 1858.

Both the lighthouse and adjacent keepers cottages were designed and engineered by David and Thomas Stevenson, for the Northern Lighthouse Board.

The foghorn, which sounded a blast every 30 seconds, was established in October 1913, and discontinued in 1987.

Lightning has sometimes struck the tower, and on several occasions the brasswork in the lantern room turned black as a result - a job indeed to clean it all again and restore it to its former brilliance.

The nearest village to the lighthouse is Longhope, three miles away, which consists of a general store, post office, church and pub (there are only three shops and two pubs on the island). Longhope is also the nearest passenger ferry terminal. The nearest car ferry operates from Lyness, six miles away.

The lighthouse and keepers' accommodation are listed as Buildings of Special Architectural and Historic Interest, and are Category 'B' listed.

The two single storey cottages which now provide self-catering accommodation were originally the Assistant Keepers' quarters. The back to back houses have a double apex roof, and both have been renovated without spoiling the traditional design of the buildings, which have Victorian sized rooms. The former Principal Keeper's

Photo: Christine Willers

cottage is situated just across the courtyard, with another smaller dwelling for use by visiting engineers and trainee keepers forming an 'L' shape adjoining the Principal Keeper's cottage.

The light was automated in 1991 and is now remotely monitored from the Northern Lighthouse Board's offices in Edinburgh.

The accommodation is set within walled grounds, but outside the perimeter walls the cliffs fall sharply to the sea below, children should be supervised at all times.

Established: 1858
Height of tower: 22 metres
Elevation of light: 35 metres
Automated: 1991
Character: 1 white flash
                      every 20 seconds
Range of light: 18 miles
Fog signal: None
Access to tower: None

31	SUMBURGH HEAD, SHETLAND

Photo: Shetland Amenity Trust

Self-catering cottage, sleeps 6

Contact:
Shetland Amenity Trust,
Garthspool, Lerwick,
Shetland ZE1 0NY
Tel: 01595 694688
Email: info@visitshetland.com
www.lighthouse-holidays.com

Off the southern headland of Shetland lies a turbulent stretch of water, the Sumburgh Roost. The name Sumburgh is thought to be derived from the Norse, Sunn Borg, or the South Broch.

With the development of trade in the 18th century, coastal traffic proceeded along the eastern side of Shetland from ports in southern Norway bound for Britain and beyond. North Atlantic trade was also becoming increasingly important, with cargoes of timber and tobacco for Europe sailing eastwards past Sumburgh Head. With this increased traffic came the inevitable need for a lighthouse, as more and more vessels were lost along the treacherous coast.

In 1815 Robert Stevenson, Engineer to the Northern Lighthouse Board, inspected the area. Building commenced in January 1819 by John Reid, a builder from Peterhead. Because of its isolated position the double thickness walls were built to keep out the damp.

During its erection, the *Freemason* of Lerwick, bound from Peterhead to Greetness with glass and materials for the lighthouse, foundered at the entrance to Greetness Voe. Only one of the crew was saved.

The tower was first lit in 1821 and contained 26 parabolic reflectors with lamps, instead of the usual 21 at that time. It originally displayed a fixed white light, visible for 24 miles at an elevation of 299ft above sea level.

On 19th January 1864 the *Royal Victoria*, a coal ship, bound from Sunderland to Calcutta foundered near the lighthouse. Of the 32 crew, 13 perished, including Captain Leslie who was buried at Dunrossness Churchyard. His parents presented a bell, to be used as a fog signal at Sumburgh Head, and this was used until the fog signal was established in 1906. The bell was removed and hung in the Parish Church at Dunrossness, where it still remains. The fog signal, which sounded one blast every 90 seconds was discontinued in 1987.

In 1871 two of the keepers were charged with conspiracy when one of them fell asleep whilst on duty. They both agreed not to report the incident, but were later found out. As a result, both the Assistant Keeper and Principal Keeper with 23 years' service, were dismissed.

Photo: Frank Turner

The lighthouse was automated in Spring 1991, and the Category B listed dwelling was bought privately in October 1993. This has since been bought by the Shetland Amenity Trust, a charitable organisation set up to conserve and enhance Shetland's heritage. The tower is located between the two dwellings and behind these, offset, is the Engine Room and a third dwelling. The local assistant's block and stores were located adjacent to these.

Sumburgh Head has been designated an Area of Special Scientific Interest, an Special Area of International Importance, and is now an official bird reserve, in agreement with the RSPB. The area is in the flight path of migrating birds, and many stop off here in spring and autumn for shelter around the walls. During the summer months puffins, guillemots, razorbills, kittiwakes and shags can be seen in abundance on the cliffs around the lighthouse.

Accommodation includes one double, one twin and a bunk bedded room. The

Photo: Frank Turner

fully equipped kitchen includes a washing machine, and the cottage is centrally heated. The dwelling is located inside a walled boundary, but outside the wall the cliffs fall steeply to the sea below, children should be supervised at all times.

Established:	1821
Height of tower:	17 metres
Elevation of light:	91 metres
Automated:	1991
Character:	3 white flashes every 30 seconds
Range of light:	23 miles
Fog signal:	None
Access to tower:	None

Photo: Keith Morton

Two self-catering cottages,
each sleeps 6

Contact:
Shetland Amenity Trust,
Garthspool, Lerwick,
Shetland ZE1 0NY
Tel: 01595 694688
Email: info@visitshetland.com
www.lighthouse-holidays.com

The six mile long island of Bressay curves parallel to the east coast Mainland of Shetland. Bressay Sound separating the island from Mainland provides a natural shelter for Lerwick and its harbour.

The lighthouse is situated on the south west of the island at Kirkabister Ness (Ness meaning headland), on a low lying shelf with the island rising up steeply behind it; from seaward its white encircling walls and buildings stand out against the greenery of the island.

Along with Out Skerries and Muckle Flugga, the lighthouse was built to serve naval traffic during the Crimean War. Application to build a lighthouse was made by the Commissioners of Northern Lights in November 1854, and approved by the Board of Trade in the same month. However, there then followed lengthy correspondence between the Board of Trade and Trinity House, who were concerned about the cost of building the new lighthouse. Much discussion took place over the plans and specifications, and building work was delayed until February 1856.

The 52ft high white tower and buildings were designed by David and Thomas Stevenson, and a light was first exhibited on 31st August 1858, the original lighting being provided by a paraffin vapour burner which was rotated by clockwork mechanism with a falling weight down the centre of the tower. Its character, a red and white alternate flash at one minute intervals, was visible in clear weather for 6 miles.

An important aspect of lighthouse keeping was good timekeeping. In July 1886 the Commissioners arrived at Bressay in fog aboard the NLB tender *Pharos* at 1.00pm. On arrival, they found the lighthouse clock stopped at 11.00am. The keepers had evidently not seen them coming!

In the summer, mornings can be light extremely early; this is known locally as the "Midsummer Dim". On one such occasion, the light was extinguished ten minutes before its official time. Unfortunately for the keepers, an observant person on the mainland had spotted the early extinction of the light and had duly

Photo: Shetland Amenity Trust

reported this to Headquarters. A few days later the Principal Keeper was reprimanded by the lighthouse Commissioners.

After its automation in 1989, the keepers' accommodation at Bressay was used as a shore station for the keepers and their families of Muckle Flugga, the most northerly lighthouse in the UK. The fog signal that had sounded 2 blasts every 90 seconds was discontinued in 1987.

Even in recent times, the treacherous coast has claimed a number of vessels. Probably the most notorious of the last few years was the grounding of the oil tanker *Braer*, which had catastrophic effects on the marine wildlife of the area. Less than a year later, in November 1993, a Latvian factory ship the *Lunokhod* also ran aground close to the lighthouse

In November 1995 the buildings were purchased by the Shetland Amenity Trust, a charitable organisation set up to conserve and enhance Shetland's heritage. The two former keepers' cottages were refurbished and now form the holiday accommodation. The complex is surrounded by a boundary wall but beyond this the cliffs fall steeply to the sea below, children should be supervised at all times.

Bressay Island is a five minute ferry ride from the main Northlink ferry terminal on Mainland Shetland - from here there are services to the other out islands and to Aberdeen.

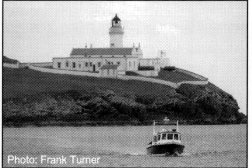

Photo: Frank Turner

Established:	1858
Height of tower:	16 metres
Elevation of light:	32 metres
Automated:	1989
Character:	2 white flashes every 20 seconds
Range of light:	23 miles
Fog signal:	None
Access to tower:	None

Photo: Shetland Amenity Trust

Self-catering cottage, sleeps 6

Contact:
Shetland Amenity Trust,
Garthspool, Lerwick,
Shetland ZE1 0NY
Tel: 01595 694688
Email: info@visitshetland.com
www.lighthouse-holidays.com

A temporary light powerful enough to give warning of the Ve Skerries reef eight and half miles offshore was erected in 1915 on the Eshaness peninsula on the north west coast of Mainland Shetland. The beacon was an iron tower, containing a lantern, machinery and an acetylene generating plant, and constructed in about two months. The building materials reached the remote location by pony and cart once they arrived on Shetland. The temporary light was removed after World War One.

The current 37ft high square white lighthouse was built in 1929 by David A Stevenson. This was the last manned lighthouse designed for the Northern Lighthouse Board by the Stevenson family of engineers, who built over a hundred lighthouses in Scotland in the preceding 150 years.

Sitting on top of a 200ft cliff, the light flashes white every 12 seconds.

At Stenness, the site of a former fishing station sheltered by Stenness Isle, is a stone cross erected by the Commissioners for Northern Lighthouses in 1927, to mark the spot where supplies for the Eshaness Lighthouse were landed.

Photo: Keith Morton

The lighthouse was built to guide ships away from the Ve Skerries. However, soon after it was established, the Aberdeen trawler *Ben Doran* was wrecked in the area and all hands were lost.

Due to heavy oil-tanker traffic bound to and from the developing Sullom Voe oil terminal, a lighthouse was built on the Ve Skerries in 1979. Eshaness was used as the construction site for the new lighthouse.

During a storm, one of the keepers reported that around 20 barrow loads of rock had been thrown onto the roof and courtyard. One of the panes of glass in the lantern were smashed, almost 200ft above sea level.

Photo: Keith Morton

Alterations were made to the light in 1974 when it was automated. The most difficult part was cutting a new entrance door to the tower, which is made of reinforced concrete. Steel chains had been embedded into the concrete, and to cut the door took almost four weeks. In the same year the light's intensity was increased to 46,500 candlepower to give the light a nominal range of 25 miles.

After automation the dwelling was sold to a private owner. It was sold twice before being bought by writer Sharma Krauskopf in 1999. The house was completely renovated to match the style of the original lighthouse keeper's accommodation. The house looks much like it would have done when built in 1929, with the exception of the kitchen which has all modern appliances.

In early 2005 the Shetland Amenity Trust purchased the property from Ms Krauskopf, and extensive maintenance was carried out. The accommodation comprises two double rooms, and one bunk bedded room. The grounds are enclosed by walls, but steep cliffs fall to the sea below, children should be supervised at all times.

Photo: Keith Morton

Established:	1929
Height of tower:	12 metres
Elevation of light:	61 metres
Automated:	1974
Character:	1 white flash every 12 seconds
Range of light:	25 miles
Fog signal:	None
Access to tower:	None

Two self-catering apartments,
each sleeps 4

Contact:
National Trust for Scotland,
Wemyss House,
28 Charlotte Square,
Edinburgh EH2 4ET
Tel: 0131 243 9594
Email: holidays@nts.org.uk
www.ntsholidays.com

The Stoer peninsula is a rocky projection some two miles wide and four miles long, pointing west out into the Minch. From Clashmore, in the centre of the peninsula, a road heads west to Stoer Head Lighthouse, which marks the most westerly point of the peninsula. One of the highlights in the area is the Old Man of Stoer, a 200ft high rock stack just south of the headland.

From 1787 to 1937, Thomas Smith, his son-in-law Robert Stevenson, and other members of the Stevenson family designed the majority of Scotland's lighthouses, often in challenging locations, including Stoer Head Lighthouse in 1870.

It was not until 1853 that regular wreck returns were kept and figures for 1859-66 showed that an average of 24 vessels a year were stranded on sands and rocks around the Scottish coast. David and Thomas Stevenson had now taken over as engineers for the Northern Lighthouse Board, and they prepared a list of 45 possible sites thought necessary to complete a system of lights around the coasts of Scotland. Stoer Head was included in this list, but it was not until 1870 that a light marking the headland of the Point of Stoer was finally

built atop a sandstone cliff.

Photo: Lorna Hunter

Although the lighthouse is relatively short (only 47ft high) its elevation above sea level is 178ft.

The lighthouse was manned by a Principal and Assistant Lightkeeper, who lived with their families at Stoer Head.

Nearby you can see the remains of the former byre, stable, cow shed, pig house and cart shed all built for life at this very remote lighthouse.

The keepers' children were educated at Stoer Public School, however there were no senior schools in the area so the children had to continue their secondary education away from the lighthouse at boarding school.

During long winter nights, the need to constantly check everything and trim the lamp wicks every four hours was extremely demanding.

The lighthouse is located 10 miles north of the fishing village of Lochinver. Most visitors to the area are attracted by the sandy white beaches of Achmelvich Bay and the Bay of Clachtoll, pink sands of Clashnessie Bay and wildlife, which includes falcons, seals and whales.

Both apartments have two twin bedded rooms. The lighthouse is surrounded by walls, but children should be supervised at all times.

Established: 1870
Height of tower: 14 metres
Elevation of light: 59 metres
Automated: 1978
Character: 1 white flash every 15 seconds
Range of light: 24 miles
Fog signal: None
Access to tower: None

Photo: Fran Cree and Chris Barrett

Bed and Breakfast,
and Hostel accommodation

Contact:
Fran Cree and Chris Barrett,
Rua Reidh Lighthouse,
Melvaig, Gairloch IV21 2EA
Tel: 01445 771263
Email: ruareidh@tiscali.co.uk
www.ruareidh.co.uk

The peninsula leading out from Gairloch ends in the headland of Rubha Reidh, affording fine views across the Minch to the Outer Hebrides and the Isle of Skye. Rua Reidh has various spellings, including Rhubh' Re, Rubha Reidh; its meaning being "Smooth Point". It was previously an area for crofting, although this is now in decline, there being much evidence of this in the ruined cottages dotted around.

Although the coast of Wester Ross is on the same latitude as Siberia and Hudson Bay, the North Atlantic Drift softens the blast of the prevailing winds, and sub-tropical plants and exotic trees flourish in nearby gardens along the coast.

The lighthouse is situated on the north west promontory of Wester Ross, at the entrance to Loch Ewe and a deep natural harbour. During the Second World War this was an important mustering area for wartime convoys.

A lighthouse was first proposed in 1853 by David Stevenson, but refused by the Board of Trade due to the cost, estimated at £5,000. In August 1906 David Stevenson recommended that there should be a major, fully manned light exhibited on a prominent headland of Ross-shire. The Northern Lighthouse Board made an application to Trinity House, but it was again refused because the cost was prohibitive. After lengthy discussions between the two organisations, Trinity House conceded, but the Board of Trade refused the application. At last, in May 1908, application was granted to erect a light and fog signal, the total cost estimated at £14,900, ironically almost three times as expensive as the original estimate.

Work eventually commenced on building the lighthouse in 1910, the work being overseen by David A Stevenson. Its light was first exhibited in January 1912, provided by a paraffin vapour burner and displayed six white flashes every 30 seconds. It now has a character of 4 white flashes every 15 seconds. The huge optic, which was one of the largest ever produced, rotated by clockwork around the light source.

The fog horn was operated by compressed air, provided by large diesel engines which powered the compressors. The clockwork mechanism controlled a valve, which timed the blasts of 4 every 90 seconds, and could be heard from 10 miles away. It was installed in 1912, and withdrawn from use in September 1980.

During a storm in 1944, the vessel *William H Welch* missed its entrance to Loch Ewe, and went ashore at Black Bay. Two of the keepers were involved in rescuing the crew by walking across a dangerous snow-covered peat bog to reach the stricken vessel, but of the 74 aboard, only 15 survived.

The original optical apparatus, fog horn and clockwork coder which controlled the compressed air emissions along with some of the lighthouse's archive material can now be found in the Gairloch Heritage Museum 12 miles away. The lens and lighting apparatus was removed in 1985 prior to its automation.

The surrounding area of Rua Reidh hosts various sea and wildlife from golden eagles to seals, dolphins, otters and whales. The local area is also strewn with archaeological remains, including Bronze and Iron Age hut circles to mesolithic caves.

Fran Cree and Chris Barrett have owned the lighthouse since 1990 when they obtained a grant and converted it into a hostel and outdoor activity centre. Both of them have experience of activity and outward bound holidays. There are various walking programmes to suit all levels of experience, from a moderate level seven day coast to coast walk to an easy level "Highlands and Islands" programme, starting at the lighthouse and visiting Lewis for several days, with walks to the famous Callanish Standing Stones and of the Butt of Lewis Lighthouse.

Photo: Fran Cree and Chris Barrett

Established:	1912
Height of tower:	25 metres
Elevation of light:	37 metres
Automated:	1986
Character:	4 white flashes every 15 seconds
Range of light:	24 miles
Fog signal:	None
Access to tower:	None

Photo: Eilean Ban Trust

Self-catering cottage, sleeps 4

Contact:
The Eilean Ban Trust,
The Pier, Kyleakin,
Isle of Skye IV41 8PL
Tel: 01599 530040
Email: enquiries@eileanban.org
www.eileanban.org

Eilean Ban Lighthouse (also known as Kyleakin), located on the island of the same name, nestles below the Skye road bridge which links Skye with the mainland; indeed the bridge is partly constructed on Eilean Ban.

Engineer David Stevenson proposed the building of the lighthouse to mark the channel between the island (then known as Gillian Island) and the Isle of Skye. His plans were accepted by the Lighthouse Commissioners in 1853, and in 1855 the island was purchased by the Northern Lighthouse Board from Alex Matheson MP for 10 guineas. Built by David and Thomas Stevenson, the 70ft tall lighthouse was completed in 1857, and first lit on 10th November of the same year. The light was originally fuelled by sperm whale oil, and the white beam was flanked by a red and green sector to indicate the safe channel.

Originally there were two lighthouse keepers resident with their families on the island, and a part time occasional keeper was on permanent standby in Kyleakin in case of illness or leave or absence.

With the introduction of a paraffin vapour lamp in 1898, the manning of the light was reduced to just one keeper and his family. Prior to the building of the Skye Bridge, the lighthouse was

Photo: Eilean Ban Trust

Photo: Eilean Ban Trust

serviced and refuelled by boat. Refuelling points were located on the north and south shore of the island as the greater depth of water allowed larger boats to berth.

In 1960 the light was changed to acetylene gas, the station automated and the lighthouse was reclassified as a minor light. The now redundant cottages were no longer needed by the Northern Lighthouse Board, and in 1963 were bought by Gavin Maxwell, naturalist, conservationist and author of "Ring of Bright Water", although he did not live on Eilean Ban full time until January 1968, after fire destroyed his cottage at Sandaig. He remained on the island until his death in September 1969. Prior to Maxwell buying the cottages, the living space was divided in two, but this was later removed, creating 40ft of space that became known as the Long Room, which is now a museum to Maxwell's life.

After Maxwell's death the cottages changed hands, and owners included actor Michael Bryant, and Kwik-Fit entrepreneur Sir Tom Farmer.

The lighthouse was discontinued in 1993 with the building of the Skye Bridge, but remains a prominent daymark. The channel into Loch Alsh was marked by red and green port and starboard lateral buoys.

Photo: Eilean Ban Trust

By 1996 the cottages had become derelict. The Eilean Ban Trust was formed, and the cottages were restored. The Bright Water Visitor Centre was established to provide education and information about the island's cultural and natural history.

Established: 1857
Height of tower: 21 metres
Discontinued: 1993
Access to tower: None

Self-catering cottage, sleeps 6

Contact:
Bill Lloyd, John and Jacqui Chapple,
Steading Holidays, Kilchoan,
Acharacle, Argyll PH36 4LH
Tel: 01972 510262
Email: westerlypoint@tiscali.co.uk
www.steading.co.uk

The Ardnamurchan peninsula juts out 35 miles north west of Oban, above the top of the island of Mull. Its unpainted pink granite lighthouse stands proudly on the most westerly point of mainland Britain, this being some 23 miles further west than Land's End in Cornwall. There are many variations of explanation for the name; "Point of the sea hounds, or otters", Airde meaning point, Muirchu meaning sea hound or otter, "Point of the pirates, or wreckers", Col coming from Muirchol, meaning wickedness, or "Point of the Great Ocean".

In 1845 20 acres of land were purchased for £20 from the landowner, Alexander Cameron to construct a lighthouse on the point. He was reluctantly paid £58 for maintenance and inconvenience caused during the building operations. The 118ft high tower was engineered by Alan Stevenson, and the building contractor was a Mr Hume. Construction took three years to complete, during which time the workmen suffered with scurvy. The granite came from the island of Mull, and was a pinkish colour compared to the grey of the local granite on the point.

When finished, only three other lights existed on the west coast of Scotland; Barra, Lismore and Skerryvore. It completed the lighting of the south of the Hebridean Sea and improved navigation between Oban and The Hebrides.

The tower and keepers' houses are now category 'A' listed, being of Architectural and Historic Interest, and are unusual in that they were built in Egyptian style. The cottages were built at the same time as the tower to house the keepers and their families. Originally two keepers were appointed, with a yearly allowance of £18. They also kept two cows and about a dozen sheep.

The light was first exhibited on 5th October 1849 and displayed a fixed white light, from an oil lamp which was visible for 18 miles.

On the morning of 22nd January 1852, during a severe storm, the tower was struck by lightning, causing broken panes and plaster to fall off the walls. 50ft of the boundary wall also collapsed, and 40ft of the road was washed away by the sea. The keepers' boat was smashed to pieces even though it was secured 15ft above the last known high water mark.

In 1928 the light was changed to a group flashing character, flashing twice every 30 seconds. The light source was upgraded to a paraffin vapour burner, which gave a very bright light, but used only a fraction of the fuel of the old oil lamp. The optic producing the flashing character had to be turned by a clockwork mechanism which needed rewinding every 1½ hours. A red sector was also exhibited from the lantern onto the dangerous rocks below.

Originally a siren fog signal operated, the main fog trumpet being situated on the cliff edge at the front of the tower. An electric fog signal replaced this, but was discontinued in June 2005. In 1997, when the visitor centre was opened, an all weather viewing area was erected close to the former fog trumpet to allow visitors to shelter in inclement weather when watching the sea for whales, dolphins and porpoises.

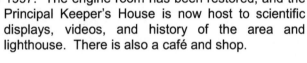

During the bicentenary of the Northern Lighthouse Board in 1986, Her Majesty The Queen, the Duke of Edinburgh, and the Duke and Duchess of York visited the lighthouse and keepers, marking a memorable occasion.

After its automation, the adjoining property was purchased in 1989, and a visitor centre was opened in June 1997. The engine room has been restored, and the

Principal Keeper's House is now host to scientific displays, videos, and history of the area and lighthouse. There is also a café and shop.

Ardnamurchan can also be reached by ferry from Tobermory on Mull, to Kilchoan, the nearest village to the lighthouse.

Established:	1849
Height of tower:	36 metres
Elevation of light:	55 metres
Automated:	1988
Character:	2 white flashes every 20 seconds
Range of light:	24 miles
Fog signal:	None
Access to tower:	Visitor centre

Self-catering cottage, sleeps 10

Contact:
Tigh Soluis Cottages,
Corran Lighthouse Lodge,
3 Melville Crescent,
Edinburgh EH3 7HW
Tel: 0131 623 5013
Email:
info@corranlighthouselodge.com
www.corranlighthouselodge.com

Stretching from Fort William to Inverness, the Caledonian Canal is 60 miles long. Twenty-two miles of which are man-made, the rest are natural lochs. The Great Glen through which the canal runs almost directly from south west to north east has for centuries been the region's natural line of communication, allowing mariners to avoid the long and often hazardous route round the north-west of Scotland and through the Pentland Firth. Started in 1803, plans were produced by Thomas Telford following survey work by James Watt some 30 years earlier. By the time the canal was opened in 1822 it had taken 17 years and cost £840,000. However, instead of the 20ft depth in Telford's plans, the canal when initially opened had only a maximum depth of 14ft, meaning that it became increasingly too shallow for the large ships being built at the time. A second phase was undertaken between 1844 and 1847.

Loch Linnhe extends to just over 9 miles and is an average of 1¼ miles wide. It opens onto the Firth of Lorn at its south western end. Situated on the shores of Loch Linnhe, 7 miles south of Fort William, Corran Lighthouse was built by David and Thomas Stevenson in 1860. It was one of a chain marking the route to the Caledonian Canal. The lighthouse exhibited a fixed white and red light from a fourth order optic at an elevation of

38ft, the white sector having a range of 10 miles. The Corran ferry crosses Loch Linnhe at the Corran Narrows. The route of this ferry lies on one of the ancient

drove routes from the Highlands to central Scotland. The eastern slipway is known as Nether Lochaber, and the western side of the crossing is guarded by the picturesque lighthouse standing on the shore with its cottages. Following the road westwards from the lighthouse a fifty mile drive will lead alongside the beautiful Loch Sunart and on to the Ardnamurchan peninsula, the most westerly point of mainland Britain. The road eventually leads to the Point of Ardnamurchan with its lighthouse and visitor centre.

In 1898 the light was converted to the less labour intensive light source of oil gas, and the lighthouse was reduced from two to one keeper and his family.

The lighthouse was automated in 1970, with further modernisation taking place in 2004, the coloured sectors being retained. The red sectors are to be avoided as these are close to the shore, whereas the green and white sectors are used to guide vessels up to Corran Point. The light has an isophase character which means the light is shown for a period equal to the length of the eclipse.

The lighthouse keepers cottages and ancillary buildings were converted into a large house with five double en-suite bedrooms plus another smaller bedroom sleeping two. The house is surrounded by a large private walled garden, which has its own access to the shore of the loch, young children should be supervised at all times.

Established:	1860
Height of tower:	13 metres
Elevation of Light:	12 metres
Automated:	1970
Character:	Isophase white/red/green every 4 seconds
Range of light:	White 10 miles Red 7 miles
Fog signal:	None
Access to tower:	None

Hynish Signal Tower

Self-catering or full board:
    Alan Stevenson House sleeps up to 24 (bunks)
    Morton Boyd House sleeps up to 8
    The Cottage sleeps up to 8

Contact: Monica Smith, Alan Stevenson House
Lower Square, Hynish, Isle of Tiree PA77 6UG
Tel: 01879 220726
Email: info@hebrideantrust.org
www.hynishcentre.co.uk

Skerryvore is a jagged rock located about 11 miles south west of Tiree, lying between the Hebrides and northern coast of Ireland. Skerryvore comes from the Gaelic sgeir (rock) and mhor (big). A large number of wrecks made the need for a lighthouse here quite urgent, and the island of Tiree was chosen as a base for the construction of Skerryvore Lighthouse, later described by Robert Louis Stevenson as "the noblest of all extant deep sea lights".

Between 1836 and 1837 quarries were opened and a pier constructed at Hynish, on the south west of Tiree. Alan Stevenson was appointed Clerk of Works for the Commissioners of Northern Lights. He proposed a wooden barrack for the workmen on the reef and persuaded the Board to build a steam tender to tow the stone lighters between the workyard and the rock. The men had only 165 hours of work on the reef in the first season, but the sixty foot barrack was constructed before it ended. However, by November, it had been washed away, and work had to start over again the following season.

Whilst work was carried out on the reef, at Hynish each stone was carefully cut and fitted in its place course by course on a platform in the work yard before being shipped to the rock. In April 1840 the third season began with over 60 masons now employed at Hynish. Over
Alan Stevenson House
20,000 cubic feet of granite was dressed and prepared between April and October. At the main quarry at Loch Loich on Mull over 2,500 blocks were cut. Sometimes as many as 95 blocks a day would be carved at Hynish, and as many as 80 craftsmen worked through the winter.

On 26th September 1843 the lighting apparatus was installed, and on 23rd November the lamp was pointed towards the lookout tower at Hynish and lit for an experimental two hours. Skerryvore was first officially lit on 1st February 1844.

Thomas Campbell was the first Signalman at Hynish. A lookout was kept between 9-10am and 2-3pm, hoping to catch a glimpse of

The Cottage

a signal from the lighthouse. A signal was acknowledged by hoisting a ball to the top of the flagstaff on the Signal Tower. If a keeper was on duty whilst his wife gave birth, the sex of the baby would be communicated by hoisting either a pair of trousers or a dress to the top of the flagstaff so the keeper would know whether he had a son or daughter.

By 1849 school teachers had been appointed to Hynish where the keepers families lived. In the summer of 1892 the Skerryvore families were moved from Hynish to join those from Dubh Artach Lighthouse on the island of Erraid, off Mull, where a dual shore station for both lighthouses was established.

On 16th March 1954, the local people of Tiree raised the alarm as they noticed that the Skerryvore Lighthouse was in flames. The keepers had escaped the burning tower, and had spent the night huddled on the rock, to be rescued the following morning. Temporary lights were established due to the extensive damage caused to the lighthouse. It was to be 1959 before the lighthouse was fully back in service.

When the Hebridean Trust was formed in 1982, the buildings beside the pier at Hynish provided limited shelter from the elements to a few local boats. Though sturdily built over 150 years earlier as part of the Skerryvore Lighthouse project, the buildings were well on their way to ruin. In partnership with the Highlands

Morton Boyd House

and Islands Development Board the Hebridean Trust put together the idea, design team and funding to create one of the biggest visitor facilities on Tiree. The excellent museum, which was originally housed in the Signal Tower has since been moved to a larger centre next to Morton Boyd House.

Self-catering, sleeps 6

Contact:
Ecosse Unique Ltd,
Lilliesleaf, Melrose,
Roxburghshire TD6 9JD
Tel: 01835 822277
www.uniquescotland.com/lochindaal

The island of Islay's population is mainly centred around the villages of Bowmore, Port Ellen and Port Charlotte. Apart from a few other smaller villages, the rest of the island is sparsely populated and mainly agricultural. Port Charlotte on the Rinns of Islay, with its whitewashed houses overlooking Loch Indaal, was founded in 1828 by Walter Frederick Campbell and named after his mother. As with other villages on Islay, Port Charlotte had a distillery, but this closed in 1929.

In the 1830s the population of the island began to decrease from its peak of 15,000 as a result of the Highland Clearances. Today's population is around 3,000. Most emigrants from Islay made new homes in Canada, USA and Australia.

The south western tip of the main island is a rocky region called The Oa. On the island there are several lochs, including Loch Indaal, a sea loch which separates the Rhinns of Islay from the rest of the island, and is formed along a branch of the great Glen Fault.

Loch Indaal light is located on the south east side of the Rinns of Islay off Scotland's south west coast. As the light is located near the town of Port Charlotte, it is often known as the Port Charlotte light. Established in 1869 the white brick tower with black lantern is still operational.

Loch Indaal was built in

Photo: www.uniquescotland.com/lochindaal

Photo: www.uniquescotland.com/lochindaal

1869 by David and Thomas Stevenson. In 1897 it was converted to oil gas, which meant that only one keeper was required. It was converted from oil to incandescent vapour in 1905.

An American memorial in the shape of a lighthouse can be seen at the Mull of Oa, on the south west tip of the island. It was created by the American Red Cross to commemorate the loss of two troop ships in 1918. The *Tuscania*, a passenger liner, was on its way from New Jersey to the coast of France with 2,000 American soldiers and a crew of more than 300. At Halifax, Nova Scotia, they joined a convoy and entered the British waters between Islay and Northern Ireland on 5th February. The convoy was followed by a German submarine U77 which torpedoed the *Tuscania*, and she sank after a few hours seven miles off the Islay coast near the Oa peninsula. An estimated 230 lives were lost. A few months later on 6th October 1918, only a few miles from the place where the *Tuscania* sank, *HMS Otranto* was carrying troops from New York to Glasgow when it collided with the steamship *HMS Kashmir* during a heavy storm.

The former keepers' house has undergone extensive renovation, and has 4 acres of land above the shore.

Photo: ALK

The village of Port Charlotte is a ten minute walk away from the lighthouse, and the neighbouring island of Jura is a 5 minute ferry ride away from Port Askaig, on the east coast of the island.

Established: 1869
Height of tower: 13 metres
Elevation of light: 15 metres
Character: 2 white/red flashes
                    every 7 seconds
Range of light: White 13 miles,
                    Red 12 miles
Fog signal: None
Access to tower: None

41 | MULL OF KINTYRE, ARGYLL AND BUTE

Two self-catering cottages,
One sleeps 4,
the other sleeps 5

Contact:
National Trust for Scotland,
Wemyss House,
28 Charlotte Square,
Edinburgh EH2 4ET
Tel: 0131 243 9594
Email@holidays@nts.org.uk
www.ntsholidays.com

In 1782 an almost uninterrupted succession of storms struck the British coasts, and in one night two herring vessels were wrecked when rounding the Kintyre peninsula, and many lives were lost. Shortly afterwards a lighthouse was established in 1788, one of the first to be erected by the Northern Lighthouse Board.

The building of the lighthouse, near the rocks known as "The Merchants of Three Pedlars", was supervised by Thomas Smith, who was appointed Engineer to the Board in 1787. The light was first exhibited on 1st November 1788.

Mull of Kintyre was a difficult site to build on, inaccessible by sea and without a road over the rough moorland. D Alan Stevenson describes the light in his book *The World's Lighthouses Before 1820*: "This lighthouse was erected on a precipitous cliff 240ft above the sea and inaccessible from it, but the rocky and desolate interior of Cantyre peninsula made the lighthouse site scarcely more accessible by land. Materials and stores had to be landed by boat 6 miles away and taken on horseback over the mountain with 1 cwt as the limited load. A single journey from landing-place to lighthouse represented one day's work. After two working seasons, the light was shown in November 1788".

The lighthouse was rebuilt in its present form around 1830. It was equipped with a siren fog signal in 1884, this gave two blasts every 4 minutes.

The *Signal*, the Northern Lighthouse Board's only steel paddle steamer, built in 1883, had the misfortune to run aground on the Mull of Kintyre in dense fog in 1895 while en route from McArthur's Head to Sanda. The lifeboats were at once launched and all on board, including one of the Commissioners, Sheriff William Ivory, were saved with most of their effects. Attempts to salvage the ship proved fruitless and she sank the next day. An official enquiry held that the ships lead should have been used to verify her position before altering course to round the Mull, and the whole question of the frequency of fog signals was opened up. It was suggested that a four minute period between blasts was too long.

In 1906 the light was altered from a fixed to a flashing light, and the intensity increased from 8,000 to 281,000 candlepower.

In 1976 an electric light was installed and, with the aid of a 3½ kilowatt electric filament lamp, the intensity was increased to 1,575,000 candlepower. The 1906 catadioptric lens, which up to this point had been rotated by clockwork mechanism requiring re-winding at regular intervals, was now turned by duplicate electric motors.

On 2nd June 1994 a Royal Air Force Chinook helicopter carrying almost all of the UK's senior Northern Ireland intelligence experts, crashed on the Mull of Kintyre in thick fog, killing all 25 passengers and 4 crew members on board. A small memorial is located on the hillside above the lighthouse.

The Mull of Kintyre lighthouse was automated in 1996, and in more recent years the electric fog signal has been discontinued.

The two cottages are called Hector's House and Harvey's House, the former is named after Hector Lamont MBE, the last Principal Keeper. Guests should be aware that the lighthouse is reached by a very steep approach road with several sharp bends, and should drive with extreme care. The cliffs fall away steeply beyond the lighthouse, and children should be supervised at all times.

Established:	1788
Present tower:	1830
Height of tower:	12 metres
Elevation of light:	91 metres
Automated:	1996
Character:	2 white flashes every 20 seconds
Range of light:	24 miles
Fog signal:	None
Access to Tower:	None

Photo: Northern Lighthouse Board

Three self-catering cottages, two sleep 6, the other sleeps 4

Contact:
Sanda Island Booking Office,
c/o Dunaskomel House,
High Askomil,
Campbeltown,
Argyll PA28 6EN
Tel: 01586 553511 / 07810 356278
Email: meg@sanda-island.co.uk
www.sanda-island.co.uk

Sanda Island is a privately owned island of 400 acres, situated off the southern tip of the Kintyre peninsula.

There had been demand for a lighthouse on the island of Sanda since the outward bound vessel *Christiana* of Glasgow, foundered, losing all hands on the nearby Pattersons Rock in 1825. The island forms the turning point into the Clyde after passing through the North Channel between Scotland and Ireland.

Trinity House proposed that the Mull of Kintyre light (established in 1788) should be moved to Sanda. However, the Commissioners of Northern Lighthouses refused this, although they were willing to mark Pattersons Rock with a beacon. It was finally decided to build on Ship Rock, a small precipitous islet on the south side of Sanda. With the rock being well over 100ft high, engineer Alan Stevenson only needed to build a short stone lighthouse. However, the keepers' accommodation was sited at shore level on the sheltered side of Ship Rock, and access from the dwellings to the tower was unique; Stevenson built two enclosed stairways up the steep face of Ship Rock. This is the only tower of this design in Scotland. The lighthouse was first lit in 1850.

The Northern Lighthouse Board's only steel paddle steamer, the 345 tonne *Signal*, built in 1883 by Caird and Co of Greenock, was wrecked on the Mull of Kintyre in dense fog on 28th September 1895 while on passage from McArthur's Head Lighthouse on Islay to Sanda. Although all on board, including one of the Commissioners, Sheriff William Ivory, were saved with most of their effects, attempts to salvage the ship proved fruitless, and she sank the next day.

In March 1946, the American liberty ship *Byron Darnton*, ran aground 100 yards south west of the lighthouse. Fifty four people were on board and all were saved. On 19th October 1970 the Dutch cattle ship *Hereford Express* ran aground. Her cargo of livestock was either drowned or destroyed by the SSPCA officers who flew out to Sanda by helicopter.

Photo: Sanda Island

The lighthouse was originally relieved by boat but in the mid 1970s helicopter reliefs were introduced to the service, which meant that generally fog or sea mist was the only cause for a delayed relief.

Sanda Island has the distinction of having the most remote public house in the British Isles. Opened in 2003, the Byron Darnton Tavern is named after the ship which ran aground in 1946.

The island is known for the ruins of a chapel built by St Ninian. Legend has it that St Ninian himself is buried on Sanda, and that death within a year will fall upon anyone who stands on his grave.

The island of Sanda can be easily viewed from the village of Southend at the southern tip of the Kintyre peninsula, and also on clear days from the Island of Arran. It is known locally on Arran as "Spoon Island" because of its resemblance to an upturned spoon when viewed from the north east. Sanda Island has had a number of different owners in its history, including Jack Bruce, of the rock group Cream, who bought the isle in 1969.

Sanda Island can be reached by boat from Campbeltown, 13 miles to the north,

an hour's journey, sailing daily in summer (or by arrangement at other times).

Established:	1850
Height of tower:	15 metres,
Elevation of light:	50 metres
Automated:	1992
Character:	1 white flash every 10 seconds
Range of light:	15 miles
Fog signal:	None
Access to tower:	None

Two self-catering cottages,
   one sleeps 2, the other sleeps 4

Contact:
Mary Turner,
Kildalloig, Campbeltown, Argyll PA28 6RE
Tel: 01586 553192
Email: marycturner@btinternet.com
www.kintyrecottages.com

The Kintyre peninsula, 40 miles long and 8 miles wide, looks out along its western side towards the Antrim Coast of Northern Ireland. Its name is derived from the Gaelic "ceann - tire", meaning land's end. About a quarter of the way up the eastern side, Island Davaar is located at the entrance to Campbeltown Loch which leads to the popular sailing and fishing centre of Campbeltown. Boats cross to Ireland from the sheltered harbour in the summer. At low tide Davaar is connected to the mainland by the Dhorlin, a bank of shingle on the southern entrance to the Loch. At high tide however, it is completely cut off. The island also marks the southern entrance of Kilbrannan Sound, the stretch of water separating Kintyre and the Island of Arran.

Davaar was known as the island of Sanct Barre (1449-1508). There are variations of the origination of the name; the modern form is believed to come from an older version, Do Bharre - thy St Barre. Its name also possibly originates from Da-Bharr, meaning double pointed island.

The lighthouse, now listed as a building of Architectural and Historic Interest, is situated on the northern tip of the island, set in 1⅓ acres of land. It was established in 1854, and designed by Northern Lighthouse Board engineers, David

and Thomas Stevenson. The building contractor was John Barr and Co, the lantern was manufactured by James Milne and Son, and the leadwork by John

Marshall. The cost of construction was estimated at around £4,000.

Today the light's character is 2 white flashes every 10 seconds, producing a 300,000 candle-power light, visible up to 23 miles. The fog signal was an electric siren with flap valve shutters producing 2 blasts every 20 seconds, but this has now been discontinued.

Two main buildings stand behind the lighthouse, the original single storey keepers' dwelling, and a more recent additional cottage. The views reach out to Kilbrannan Sound and Arran.

The lighthouse is a 66ft high white tower, where a mercury vapour lamp in conjunction with catoptric mirrors was driven by clockwork machinery. Originally a revolving light was installed, producing one flash every 30 seconds, visible from 17 miles. Today the light is produced via electric sealed-beam units.

The cottages share a walled enclosure with the neighbouring caretaker. Beyond the wall the cliffs fall away steeply, and children should be supervised at all times. The cottages are connected to the mainland by the Dhorlin, which is accessible for around 3 hours either side of low tide. On arrival and departure, guests are ferried by Land Rover across the causeway, leaving their cars at the

quayside on the mainland. To walk from the lighthouse over the causeway to the mainland takes about 30 minutes.

Established:	1854
Height of tower:	20 metres
Elevation of light:	37 metres
Automated:	1983
Character:	2 white flashes every 10 seconds
Range of light:	23 miles
Fog signal:	None
Access to tower:	None

Two self-catering cottages,
one sleeps 5, the other sleeps 6

Contact:
Cottages4You
Spring Mill, Earby,
Barnoldswick BB94 0AA
Tel: 08700 782100
Email:contact@holidaycottagesgroup.com
www.cottages4you.co.uk

Heading south from Dunoon along the shores of the Firth of Clyde are the villages of Innellan and Toward. Toward is home to several historic sites including Toward Castle, which dates back to the 15th century and was the scene of the massacre of 200 Lamont clansmen by the Campbells in 1646.

Various discussions took place between the Cumray Lighthouse Trust, which later developed into the Clyde Lighthouses Trust, on the location of where their lighthouses should be situated. The Trustees had been called upon to consider better lighting of the Firth from Little Cumbrae Island up to Greenock. One strong campaign was for the building of a lighthouse on Strone Point, the division between Loch Long and the Holy Loch. The people of Rothesay however, pressed for the establishment of a lighthouse on Toward Point (also known then as Towart Point).

At a meeting of the Trustees in Glasgow on 10th August 1795, the Chair reported: "On the 3rd of last month the Committee inspected the Towart Point, and they are clearly of opinion that the erection of a light house as recommended by some of the Rothesay people would serve no other good end but occasionally to assist vessels going into the Harbour and might be detrimental to the general navigation of the Firth."

It was decided that there was to be no special lighting of Fairlie Roads beyond the provision of extra buoys. A new lighthouse was to be established at Cloch Point and not on the Gantocks or on Strone Point. However, later the Trust went back on the Committee's somewhat brusque dismissal of the claims of Toward.

The decision of the Trustees to build their third major light on Toward Point was a curious reversal of policy. The committee of the early 1790s had dismissed the notion as being a sort of whim of the magistrates of Rothesay on the Isle of Bute. The switch back to Toward was almost certainly made on the advice of shipmasters that the Trust regularly consulted.

The largest ships in those days were under sail only. Having easily cleared the Cumbrae Light (re-sited by Thomas Smith and Robert Stevenson in 1793), the inward-bound navigator would naturally look for a mark ahead. The Cloch Light would be obscured from his vision for a variety of reasons. A good light on Toward would give the navigator a bearing for a good nine miles up the Firth until Cloch was in clear view and he could safely turn to starboard by the beacon towards the anchorage off Greenock.

Toward lighthouse was first lit in 1812, and designed by Robert Stevenson. There are very few records dating back to the time the lighthouse was built, but it is understood that James Lamont of Knockdow, a nearby land owner and forebear of the existing James Lamont and Sons Ltd, of Port Glasgow, supplied the labour, timber and stone for the building.

The ground was on the territory of the Lamonts of Knockdow, the hereditary Lairds of this corner of Argyll. However in 1865 the Lighthouse Trustees discovered to their alarm that they had no title to it, and hastened to secure a Feu Charter from James Lamont, then MP for Bute, at £8 per acre.

A small building on the water's edge housed the compressed air fog signal, but this is no longer operational. In 1969 the lighthouse was converted from a paraffin vapour light to fully electric automatic operation. Lighthouse Cottage, built in 1812 adjoins the tower, and Middle Cottage, built in 1934 is adjacent to

the lighthouse. Access to the cottages is along an unmade track.

Established:	1812
Height of tower:	19 metres
Elevation of light:	21 metres
Automated:	1969
Character:	1 white flash every 10 seconds
Range of light:	22 miles
Fog signal:	None
Access to tower:	None

Hotel accommodation in main building, plus five suites within the grounds

Contact:
Corsewall Lighthouse Hotel,
Kirkcolm, Stranraer DG9 0QG
Tel: 01776 853220
Email: info@lighthousehotel.co.uk
www.lighthousehotel.co.uk

On the north west tip of the Rhinns of Galloway, Corsewall Lighthouse quietly stands guard over the ferries traversing between Stranraer and Belfast. Deep-cut rock fissures bring waves battering up in spray on this jagged and dangerous coastline. Unique rock forms can be found here, and close to the lighthouse is the Iron Age fort of Dunskirkloch.

The name Corsewall is thought to be derived from "place of the cross", or "well of the cross".

Application for a light to be exhibited on Corsill Point, as it was then known, was made to the Board of Trade at Clyde in 1814 by Kirkman Finley in response to the increase in shipping trade from Greenock, Glasgow and Liverpool. The Northern Lighthouse Board approved the application the following year.

Set in twenty acres of land, the 112ft lighthouse was engineered by Robert Stevenson. It is an unusual design, with a castellated collar about a third of the way up the tower which may indicate that originally the plan was for a much shorter lighthouse.

A revolving light consisting of metal parabolic reflectors with Argand oil lamps was first lit in 1817. In 1892 a revolving optic was installed, changing the character to alternate red and white flashes every minute, its range being extended from 16 to 20 miles.

The optic sits on a roller bearing, and when installed in the late 1800s would originally have been rotated by clockwork mechanism, with a weight descending down the centre of the tower. Now it is driven by an electric motor with a backup motor in case of failure. An emergency flashing lantern with a 250-300mm polycarbonate lens and 60 watt lamp controlled with an electronic flasher is installed outside on the gallery handrail.

The foghorn gave four blasts every 90 seconds but has since been discontinued. The old red trumpet which was previously used still stands in front of the lighthouse staring silently out to sea.

Shortly after the light was first shown, it is recorded that the revolving apparatus had stopped when the Principal Keeper fell asleep whilst on watch. He was suspended from duty, but later sent to Bell Rock Lighthouse, and demoted to Assistant Keeper.

Damage was sustained in November 1970 when a trial flight by Concorde broke several panes of glass in the lantern room as it made its flypast. It flew past many times after, but no further damage was recorded.

The lighthouse was automated in 1994, and the keepers' accommodation sold privately in 1995. The reception, bar, restaurant and six bedrooms are located in the main part of the hotel, which is the former keepers' dwelling. For guests seeking further privacy there are five luxurious suites located nearby (two have

been recently built, the others are in converted outbuildings).

Established:	1817
Height of tower:	34 metres
Elevation of light:	34 metres
Automated:	1994
Character:	5 white flashes every 30 seconds
Range of light:	22 miles
Fog signal:	None
Access to tower:	None

Three self-catering cottages,
two sleep 4, the other sleeps 6

Contact:
National Trust for Scotland,
Wemyss House,
28 Charlotte Square,
Edinburgh EH2 4ET
Tel: 0844 493 2100
Email: holidays@nts.org.uk
www.ntsholidays.com

In 1828 construction started on a lighthouse at the Mull of Galloway, Scotland's most southerly point. Designed by Northern Lighthouse Board engineer Robert Stevenson, it was first lit in 1830 and showed an intermittent, or occulting light, made by moving two opaque cylindrical shades up and down to obscure the light at fixed intervals, with periods of darkness shorter than those of light. The cost of this lighthouse was around £9,000. The contractor responsible for the building was Brebner and Scott of Edinburgh.

In the early 1900s a fog siren was installed, producing two blasts every 3 minutes. This was altered in 1920 to two blasts every one and a half minutes. The fog signal has since been discontinued.

During the Second World War, on 8th June 1944 at 7.30pm a Beaufighter aircraft crashed into the lighthouse stores building. It was foggy at the time, and two men were killed as part of the roof was blown off.

Originally powered by Argand oil lamps, these were later replaced by a paraffin vapour burner until in 1971 when Mull of Galloway was converted to mains electricity. Now the light is produced using a sealed-beam unit, mounted on a gearless revolving pedestal, using a low-voltage rotary mechanism, producing a good beam for a very low power input and being sealed in a vacuum. These do not deteriorate or tarnish.

Experience had shown that the high walls built for shelter caused 'strong whirls of wind' in the courtyard around the lighthouse and interfered with the keepers' lookout. As a consequence, in 1907, the walls were lowered.

One of the outhouses within the complex originally housed the workmen who built the lighthouse. This was later extended to act as a byre (cowshed) for the lighthouse keepers. The derelict building was restored, and is now used as a visitor centre, renovated to blend in with its surroundings. The centre is run jointly by South Rhinns Community Development Trust and the RSPB. The recently built Gallie Craig Coffee House, a quarter of a mile from the lighthouse, affords excellent views of the westerly seascape towards the Irish coast.

The lighthouse is reached via dramatic forest and mountain scenery, and nearby are unspoilt sandy beaches, historic ruined castles and quaint harbour villages such as Portpatrick and Port Logan. The former keepers' cottages are situated within an RSPB reserve, with plenty of opportunity for birdwatching. The grounds

are enclosed by walls, but steep cliffs fall away beyond these, and children should be supervised at all times.

Established:	1830
Height of tower:	26 metres
Elevation of light:	99 metres
Automated:	1988
Character:	1 white flash every 20 seconds
Range of light:	28 miles
Fog signal:	None
Access to tower:	Visitor centre

Two self-catering cottages, each sleeps 4

Contact:
Linda Van Hooven
Derby House, College Green
Castletown, Isle of Man
Tel: 01624 824033
Email: lindavanhooven@iom.com
www.isle-of-man-holiday.com

Langness Point sits on a narrow low-lying peninsula that juts out from Castletown on the south east of the Isle of Man, reaching into the Irish Sea, forming two natural refuges for Castletown and Derbyhaven. The name Langness is said to mean Long Point. Rapid tides run around here, and a reef called the Skerrances is concealed off the Point.

Robert Stevenson had visited Langness in 1801 and recommended that a light be built here. In 1811 an unlit tower was built in the centre of the peninsula, which became known as the Herring Tower, but this did not prevent further shipwrecks. Despite there being over 40 shipwrecks recorded after the tower was built, Trinity House rejected all representations for a lighthouse to be built.

In 1850 a beacon was erected at Fort Island in Derbyhaven. Initially this was lit only during the herring season to guide the fishermen back to Castletown, but later it was exhibited throughout the year. However, by 1860 the local community could no longer afford to keep it lit every night, so once again it was only displayed during the fishing season.

In August 1874 experiments were undertaken at the newly completed Chicken Rock Lighthouse off the Calf of Man, to show a warning over Langness with a sector light. But at 8 miles distant Chicken Rock proved inappropriate for marking Langness. Finally in 1877 Trinity House gave the Commissioners of Northern Lighthouses their sanction to build a lighthouse at Langness Point.

Lighthouse engineers David and Thomas Stevenson designed the lighthouse and proposed a 50ft high tower, an engine house for the fog signal, houses for three keepers, outhouses including coal cellars, oil cellars, a workshop, and garden amounting to approximately 2½ acres enclosed with a stone wall. Two boat landings were also built, one to the south at Dreswick, and one to the north, overlooking Castletown.

It was to be another year before building could commence due to delays in acquiring the land, but despite this the lighthouse was completed ahead of schedule and first lit in December 1880 displaying a white flashing light every 5 seconds. The fog signal originally gave a blast every 40 seconds, this was later altered to two blasts every 60 seconds, but was finally discontinued in 1987.

On 12th December 1933 a fire broke out in the lantern, destroying the lamps. The keeper on duty claimed that he had been on the toilet when the fire had broken out. Following this fire it was decided to upgrade the lighting apparatus, and in October 1937 a new optic mounted on a mercury float was installed. The character of the light was altered to one flash every 10 seconds.

In 1994, with a reduction to the range of the light, the status of the lighthouse was regraded to a minor light, and the station became the last of the Isle of Man lights to be automated in 1996.

Accommodation is in the East and West cottages. The grounds are enclosed by walls, but children should be supervised at all times.

Established: 1880
Height of tower: 19 metres
Elevation of light: 23 metres
Automated: 1996
Character: 2 white flashes
                      every 30 seconds
Range of light: 12 miles
Fog signal: None
Access to tower: None

Bed and Breakfast accommodation

Contact:
Fiona Kilpatrick,
Great Orme Lighthouse,
Marine Drive, Great Orme's Head,
Llandudno LL30 2XD
Tel: 01492 876819
Email: enquiries@lighthouse-llandudno.co.uk
www.lighthouse-llandudno.co.uk

During the time of the industrial revolution, coastal traffic passing the north Wales coast on its way to and from Liverpool was increasing at a rapid pace. The port of Liverpool served the north west of England, Ireland and beyond, across the Atlantic.

In 1810 a signalling station was set up on Holyhead Mountain by the merchants of Liverpool, and between 1826 and 1829 this was added to by a complete chain of telegraph signals, the Great Orme being part of this. These telegraphs could send news of arrivals and departures of vessels from one end to the other. The original station was located on the summit, but was moved to the lighthouse when it was constructed. The Telegraph Room was located on the first storey at the front of the building. The room still has the telescope ports in the windows, and the equipment was still in place in 1979.

The lighthouse, an unusual square, two storey castellated structure, 37ft high, was built in 1862 and designed by George F Lyster, Engineer-in-Chief of the Mersey Docks and Harbour Board. A fixed white light was first exhibited on 1st December 1862. It had an elevation of 325ft above sea level with a red sector marking the Hoyle Bank. The arrangements of the red prisms, so constructed as to utilise wasted light from the main lamp, was the first to be used on an optic of the first order. The original light used colza oil, and later paraffin wick-lamps, which were replaced by vapourising petroleum mantle-burners in 1904. The light was visible for 24 miles in good weather. In 1923 this was replaced by dissolved acetylene mantle-lamps, producing 13,000 candle power, changing the light to unmanned status, although a keeper was kept on as a caretaker. Its character produced four white flashes every 30 seconds in the form of the morse signal B: one long flash followed by three short flashes. The white sector was shown through 144°, and the red sector through 8°. On exceptionally clear nights, the light could be seen from Snaefell in the Isle of Man, 54 miles away.

Inside the entrance hall on either side stand two 20ft high wooden pitch-pine partitions, curving out from the walls and gallery above. Originally there was a kitchen and sitting room on either side of the hallway for the keepers. Through the hallway, the Watch Room housed Decca navigation equipment. The ground floor lantern and engine room were situated behind this, with a superb panoramic view out to sea from Wirral and beyond.

The lighthouse remained in the Mersey Docks and Harbour Board's authority until 1973 when it was handed over to Trinity House. Ron Brett was keeper at the station from 1969, and promoted to Principal Keeper with his wife Gladys as Assistant Keeper when the station was handed over to Trinity House. A number of modifications were made after Trinity House took over, including white rendering, which was applied in 1974, but this has now been removed to reveal the original limestone masonry.

The light was finally switched off on 22nd March 1985, and the ensign removed in a Trinity House ceremony on 29th April 1985 by Captain PM Edge of Trinity House and Captain KJ Lewis on behalf of the Mersey Docks and Harbour Board, to whom the lease then reverted. The last keeper, Ken Chapman was present at the ceremony.

The first order dioptric lens with lamp changer and timing mechanism from the original light can now be seen in the museum at the summit of the Great Orme, which can be accessed by trams from Llandudno.

Accommodation is available in three double rooms; the Lantern Room includes the former lantern room as a lounge. Above this is the Telegraph Room from where a permanent watch was kept, and the Principal Keeper's Room, also on the first floor has views to the east.

Established:	1862
Height of tower:	11 metres
Discontinued:	1985
Access to tower:	Part of accommodation

Two self-catering cottages,
each sleeps 6
Note: Fog signal is still operational and
may sound without warning.

Contact:
Menai Holidays,
Greenfield Terrace, Hill Street,
Menai Bridge, Anglesey LL59 5AY
Tel: 01248 717135
Email: let@menaiholidays.co.uk
www.menaiholidays.co.uk

With the expansion of the port of Liverpool in the second half of the eighteenth century, the need for the seaward approaches to the city to be well marked became apparent. In 1779 the Liverpool Pilotage Service established a combined lighthouse and pilot station in an old farmhouse on the Eilian peninsula. This peninsula, about half a mile in length, was chosen as the pilot station for the Port of Liverpool as it would afford some shelter to the pilots as they boarded their cutters to take them out to the larger vessels wishing to approach the city. As a secondary service a lighthouse was incorporated into the converted farmhouse. It is likely that two fixed lights were shown from a window on either side of the farmhouse.

The light continued to operate in this way for over 50 years until in 1834 Alan Stevenson suggested to the Liverpool Trustees that the existing farmhouse be demolished and a new 70ft tower be erected. This extra elevation would allow the light to be seen from all points to seaward. The Trustees realised the light needed improving but built a new lighthouse on the highest part of the headland, designed by Board Engineer Jesse Hartley. As the headland was already 127ft above sea level, a tower was not needed to elevate the light. A 37ft high structure was erected with the lantern at ground level. Above this was a pilot lookout. Castellated walls enclosed the whole site with a gateway in the southern wall. Behind the lighthouse a large keepers dwelling was constructed with access to the tower.

A telegraph system linking the ports of Holyhead and Liverpool had been established by the Trustees in 1827. This was a line of sight semaphore system requiring nine relay stations between the two ports, and a station was established at Llaneilian, just over a mile to the south of the lighthouse.

The light housed 13 lamps and reflectors, and the flash was produced by shutter boards, which were turned by clockwork machinery. This machinery took 20 minutes to wind, then operated for 4 hours. The original lantern was replaced in 1874 by a cast iron lantern, which is still in place today. Four years later the reflectors were replaced by the current optic, produced by Chance Brothers of Birmingham. The old shutter board system was replaced by a clockwork hood which was lowered over the light for two seconds in every ten.

In 1879 the lighthouse accommodation was extended due to the decision to close the telegraph on Llaneilian, and transfer the signallers to a new electric telegraph housed at the lighthouse.

In 1948 an acetylene fog gun was installed, producing a single explosive blast every 90 seconds. Generators were installed in 1952 to provide a 100 volt electricity supply, making the Victorian clockwork mechanism obsolete, and this was removed.

On 2nd April 1973 control of the lighthouse passed from the Mersey Docks and Harbour Board to Trinity House, who also took control of the nearby Great Orme's Head lighthouse. This was now classed as a keeper and wife station. A new fog signal was installed giving one blast every 45 seconds.

When Point Lynas was fully automated in 1990 the keepers' dwellings were returned to the Mersey Docks and Harbour Board, with Trinity House now leasing access to the lamp room and a couple of other ancillary rooms. The three cottages were sold in 2000, and have been fully restored.

Accommodation is in the two former keepers dwellings. The complex is surrounded by walls, but beyond these the cliffs fall away steeply, and children should be supervised at all times.

Established:	1779
Present tower:	1835
Height of tower:	11 metres
Elevation of light:	39 metres
Automated:	1990
Character:	White occulting every 10 seconds
Range of light:	20 miles
Fog signal:	1 blast every 45 seconds
Access to tower:	None

Point Lynas, Anglesey
East and West Keepers Cottages

These former lighthouse keepers dwellings can accommodate
a party of either 6 or 12 people in two cottages.
Beautifully presented and in an outstanding, breathtaking location
with ocean views, whatever the weather.
A mass of flora and fauna, porpoises, dolphins, birds, carpets of wild flowers in the spring.
A unique opportunity to stay in a Lighthouse Keepers cottage at a working lighthouse.

50 | ST ANN'S OLD LIGHT, PEMBROKESHIRE

Two self-catering apartments,
     one sleeps 5, the other sleeps 8
Note: Fog signal at the low light is still operational and may sound without notice.

Contact:
Tot & Tann Thomas,
Elizabeth Venmore Court, Yorke Street,
Milford Haven, Pembrokeshire SA73 2LL
Tel: 01646 693331
Email:stannoldlight@aol.com
www.theoldlighthouse.co.uk

By the late 1950s Milford Haven had become Britain's biggest oil port. The approach to Milford Haven is reached through difficult and treacherous channels, and visibility can be obscured by various headlands on approach.

The site of the operational lighthouse at St Ann's reveals very little of its former history. It is the location of one of the oldest lighthouses in Britain. The earliest light was thought to be that of a chapel, St Ann's, dating back to the middle ages, built to commemorate the landing of Henry Tudor. The original light consisted of a coal brazier, tended to by a monk or hermit. When Henry VIII dissolved the monasteries in 1536, the church light was extinguished, and it was not relit again until 1660. Local merchants were granted permission from Trinity House to collect voluntary payment from passing ships towards the maintenance of the light, but permission was withdrawn in 1667 by the Corporation after the merchants were accused of extortion. The light went out once more.

Joseph Allen the landowner was granted a lease by Trinity House some time later, and in 1713 two leading lights were built, which, when kept in line would guide ships clear of Linney Head, Angle and the Crow and Toes rocks.

After much disagreement and negotiation, two new lights were completed in 1800, designed by Captain Joseph Huddart and Samuel Wyatt, Consultant Engineer to Trinity House. New dwellings were also needed. The new towers both housed Argand oil lamps, one with 16 silvered copper reflectors, the other with 11, and this new form of lighting vastly improved their visibility.

In 1814 control for the two lighthouses reverted back to Trinity House. By 1838 the low light was in danger of being undermined as the cliffs were eroding. A new light replaced it in 1844, which is the current operational lighthouse. This was designed by Trinity House Chief Engineer James Walker. The two lights each displayed a fixed white light, which were visible from a range of 18 miles.

Only 42ft in height, perched 157ft above sea level, the operational low light is not easily obscured by fog. It was electrified in 1958, and a white light flashes once every 5 seconds, with a red sector light which shines out onto the Crow and Toes Rocks. The station was automated in 1998.

The original keepers' dwellings attached to the low light were demolished, and new accommodation was built in their place during the 1950s.

The old high light operated until 1910. At the start of the Second World War the lantern on the high light was removed and an imposing, flat lookout was built, which was used by the Coastguard until 1993, when the operation moved to Milford Haven. Original fittings still appear in the old lighthouse, including the radar scanner once used by the Coastguard.

In 1967 a new low light was established on the site of the Mid Channel Rocks to the south of the headland to assist the entrance of large tankers.

One of the two holiday apartments includes accommodation within the old tower, which houses the observation lounge at the top. The second, self-contained apartment has its own private access.

Established:	1713
Present tower:	1800
Height of tower:	23 metres
Discontinued:	1910
Access to tower:	Part of accommodation

Four self-catering cottages,
each sleeps 5

Contact:
Rural Retreats,
Draycott Business Park,
Draycott, Moreton-in-Marsh,
Glos GL56 9JY
Tel: 01386 701177
Email: info@ruralretreats.co.uk
www.ruralretreats.co.uk

Nash Lighthouse was designed by Joseph Nelson, Engineer-in-Chief to Trinity House, in 1832 to mark the sandbanks off the point at the entrance to the Bristol Channel. The decision to build it followed a public outcry after the passenger steamer *Frolic* was wrecked with heavy loss of life in 1830. The final application to build two lighthouses was made in February 1830 by Thomas Protheroe, together with 439 owners and masters from the Bristol Channel ports.

Two circular stone towers were built. The eastern, or high lighthouse being 121ft high and the western or low lighthouse 82ft high. Placed 990ft apart they provided leading lights to indicate safe passage past the notorious Nash Sands, stretching eight miles westward from the Point. The high light was painted with black and white bands and the low light was white. Originally both towers showed a fixed light which was either red or white depending on the direction from which a vessel approached. The red sector shone over the Sands.

The original illumination consisted of double rows of reflectors, 13 Argand oil lamps in the high light, and 12 in the low light. The original lanterns were glazed with rectangular panes. New helically framed lanterns (with diagonal framing) were fitted to both towers in 1867.

A siren fog signal was established in 1904, this gave four blasts every 90

seconds. The fog signal building, with two massive horns protruding from the roof is located mid-way between the two towers. The fog signal engines were replaced in 1968, and the character altered to two blasts every 45 seconds. Though now discontinued as a navigational aid, the fog signal is still in working order, and on special occasions is sounded by the Attendant.

The low light was discontinued in 1923, and in the high light the reflectors were replaced with a fixed optic exhibiting a white and red occulting light. The lantern of the low light was not removed until 1955 when it was noted to be in a very dangerous condition.

The two black bands on the high light were removed in 1959 leaving a striking white tower, and in 1963 the lighthouse was connected to the mains electricity supply. During modernisation work at the lighthouse in 1968, the main light character was altered to 2 white and red flashes every 10 seconds. In 1977 a very rare tuberous thistle (Cirsium Tuberosum) was discovered growing close to the lighthouse.

Nash Point was the last manned lighthouse in Wales, and up to its automation in 1998, was the monitoring centre for Flatholm and Mumbles Lighthouses. Since automation all lights are monitored from the Trinity House Operations Control Centre in Harwich.

After automation a smaller polycarbonate panelled lens was installed to provide the main light, however, the 1923 lens has been retained on station, and is now located in one of the rooms lower down the tower.

Established:	1832
Height of tower:	37 metres
Elevation of light:	56 metres
Automated:	1998
Character:	2 white/red flashes every 15 seconds
Range of light:	White 21 miles, Red 16 miles
Fog signal:	None
Access to tower:	Visitor centre

Bed and Breakfast accommodation

Contact:
Frank & Danielle Sheahan,
West Usk Lighthouse,
Lighthouse Road, St Brides
Wentlooge, Nr Newport NP10 8SF
Tel: 01633 810126
Email:info@westusklighthouse.co.uk
www.westusklighthouse.co.uk

By the end of the 19th century, Newport was one of the busiest cargo handling centres in Britain, eventually becoming the largest port in the world handling coal shipments.

The earliest recorded application for a lighthouse to be built on the site was made in 1807, and this was renewed in 1820 when the application was finally successful. Despite its current location, the lighthouse originally stood on an island. However, by 1850 Trinity House had acquired the land from Lord Tredegar's estate and reclaimed it, joining it to the mainland.

West Usk Lighthouse is an usual design, the first to be built by James Walker (1781 - 1862), a Scottish-born architect and Consultant Engineer to Trinity House.

The lighthouse was completed in 1821 with a short tower, rising from the centre of a squat two-storey drum-shaped building. The rooms in the circular dwelling were for the use of the two keepers and their families.

The tower was 57ft high, and a fixed light was first exhibited on 1st December 1821, which had white and red sectors. The red sector shone over the Welsh Grounds and Welsh Hook sandbanks. In 1868 alterations were made, and it is likely that a helically framed lantern with diagonal framing was installed at this time. Records in 1895 and

1902 describe the light as having a triple occulting light every 30 seconds, also showing red and green sectors, visible from 11 miles.

The lighthouse was discontinued in 1922 and sold privately for £670. After 1930 it was abandoned, and fell into disrepair for many years, and at some stage the lantern was removed. By 1967 the lighthouse had been refurbished by a local man, but by the 1980s it had fallen vacant again.

In 1987 Frank and Danielle Sheahan purchased the building for £80,000 after moving from Kent. At this stage the building was derelict and vandalised, and cattle had been allowed to roam freely inside. It took four years to restore.

A new lantern was added in Christmas 1997 after much research by the owners, and funding contributions from CADW, Newport Borough Council and the Welsh Tourist Board. On 1st December 2005 the owner installed and re-lit a new modern light, although this is not recognised as a navigation aid.

West Usk is located quite close to Tredegar House. In the 17th century, the

pirate Captain Morgan was believed to have built a tunnel between the House and the site where the lighthouse is located, and contraband stored within. In the lighthouse plans, the foundations were found to be as deep as the tower is high, but there was no evidence of tunnels.

Established: 1821
Height of tower: 17 metres
Discontinued: 1922
Access to tower: Available
                    to guests

APPENDIX 1:
LIGHTHOUSE ACCOMMODATION
OUTSIDE THE UK

ARGENTINA

Punta Delgada Lighthouse
Patagonia Argentina, Peninsula
Valdés, Argentina
Tel: 2965 458444
Email: faro@puntadelgada.com
www.puntadelgarda.com/En/
ElLugarFaroPuntaDelgada.htm

AUSTRALIA

Bathurst Point, Western Australia
Two self-catering cottages,
one sleeps 4, one sleeps 6
Rottnest Island Authority,
PO Box 693, Fremantle WA 6959
Tel: 08 9432 9111
Email:
reservations@rottnestisland.com
www.rottnestisland.com

Cape Borda, South Australia
Two self-catering cottages, sleep 6
and 2, small hut sleeps 2
Flinders Chase
National Park, PMB 246,
via Kingscote 5223 Australia
Tel: 08 8559 7235
Email:
kiparksaccom@saugov.sa.gov.au

Cape Bruny, Tasmania
Self-catering cottage, sleeps 6
Tel: 03 6298 3114

Cape Byron, New South Wales
Two self-catering cottages,
one sleeps 4, one sleeps 6

Elders R Gordon & Son, PO Box 40,
Byron Bay, NSW 2481 Australia
Tel: 02 6685 6552
www.nationalparks.nsw.gov.au/
npws.nsf/Content/Accommodation

Cape Capricorn, Queensland
Self-catering, sleeps 12.
Tel: 07 4125 3447

Cape du Couedic, South Australia
Three self-catering cottages, each
sleeps 6
Flinders Chase National Park, PMB
246, via Kingscote 5223 Australia
Tel: 08 8559 7235
Email:
kiparksaccom@saugov.sa.gov.au

Cape Don, Northern Territory
Two cottages, sleeps 12
Tel: 08 8979 0030
Email:capedon@altnews.com.au
www.ozhorizons.com.au/nt/darwin/
capedon/capedon.html

Cape Leveque, Western Australia
Camping
Kooljaman at Cape Leveque,
PMB 8, Cape Leveque, Via Broome,
WA 6725 Australia
Tel: 08 9192 4970
Email: leveque@bigpond.com
www.kooljaman.com.au

Cape Naturaliste, Western Australia
Two 3 bedroom cottages, visitor centre
Sleeps 8 in bunk beds.
Tel: 08 9755 3955

www.geographebay.com
Email: lighthouse@geographebay.com

Cape Otway, Victoria
Two double studios or cottage.
Sleeps 2-16
Paul Thomson, PO Box 41, Apollo
Bay, VIC 3233 Australia
Tel: 03 5237 9240
Email: keeper@lightstation.com
www.lightstation.com

Cape Otway   Photo: Paul Thomson

Cape Schank, Victoria
Two self catering cottages
Tony Sheer, 1440 Dandenong Road,
Oakleigh, VIC 3166, Australia
Tel: 613 9568 6411
Email: lamp@austpacinns.au.com
www.austpacinns.com.au

Cape Willoughby, South Australia
Flinders Chase National Park,
PMB 246, via Kingscote 5223 Australia
Tel: 08 8559 7235
Email:
kiparksaccom@saugov.sa.gov.au

Gabo Island, Victoria
Self-catering cottage sleeps 8
Parks Victoria, Gabo Island Australia
Tel: 03 5161 9500
Email: infor@parks.vic.gov.au
www.parkweb.vic.gov.au

Green Cape, New South Wales
Two self-catering cottages,
each sleeps 6
NSW National Parks, PO Box 656,
Merimbula, NSW 2548
Tel: 02 6495 5000
Email: eden.district@npws.nsw.gov.au
www.nationalparks.nsw.gov.au/
npws.nsf/Content/Accommodation

Low Head, Tasmania
Self-catering in nearby Pilot Station
Tel: 0417 503 292
Email: pilotstation@lowhead.com

Norah Head, New South Wales
Self-catering
Bush Street, Norah Head,
NSW 2263 Australia
Tel: 02 4385 4430
Email: info_thecoast@bigpond.com
www.visitcentralcoast.com.au

Point Hicks, Victoria
Two self-catering cottages,
each sleeps 10
Point Hicks Lightstation, PO Box 122,
Cann River, VIC 3890 Australia
Tel: 03 5158 4268
Email: pointhicks@bigpond.com
www.pointhicks.com.au

Point Lowly, South Australia
Two self-catering cottages
Uniting Church
Tel: 08 8645 0436

She Oak Point and
Middle Channel Lights, Tasmania
Self-catering cottages
C/-5 Bathurst Street, George Town,
Tasmania 7253 Australia
Tel: 03 6382 1399
Email:
tamar.firstnational@bigpond.com

Smoky Cape, New South Wales
Bed & Breakfast, Self catering
Wendy and Pat Halverson,
Lighthouse Road, Arakoon, PO Box
304, South West Rocks,
NSW 2431 Australia
Tel: 02 6566 6301
Email: smokycapelighthouse@tsn.cc
www.smokycapelighthouse.com

Sugarloaf Point, New South Wales
Self-catering
Kinka Road, Seal Rocks NSW 2423
Tel: 02 4997 6590
Email:stay@
sealrockslighthouseaccommodation.au
www.srla.com.au

Swan Island, Tasmania
Self-catering
Tel: 03 6357 2211
Email: paradiserentals@bigpond.com

Troubridge Island, South Australia
Self-catering cottage, sleeps 10
Judy and Chris Johnson,
4 Blanche Street, Edithburgh, 5583,
South Australia
Tel: 08 8852 6290

Vlamingh Head, Western Australia
Ningaloo Lighthouse Caravan Park,
PO Box 504, Exmouth, WA 6707
Tel: 08 9949
Email@lighthouse@nwc.net.au
www.ningaloolighthouse.com

Wilson's Promontory, Victoria
*Dormitory style accommodation
for up to 27 people in 3 cottages.*
Wilsons Promontory National Park,
Tidal River, VIC 3960 Australia
Tel: 1800 350 552
Email: wprom@parks.vic.gov.au
www.parkweb.vic.gov.au

Andros Lighthouse
Yacht Club, Marina and apartments
Andros Lighthouse
Yacht Club and Marina,
Fresh Creek,
Andros, Bahamas
Tel: 242 368 2305
Email: relax@androslighthouse.com
www.androslighthouse.com

Bird Rock
Landrail Point,
Crooked Island,
Bahamas
Tel: 242 344 2507
Email: info@birdrocklighthouse.com
www.birdrocklighthouse.com

Palmetto Point
David E Steigelman,
1942-101 Tara Court Greenville,
NC 27858, Bahamas
Tel: 252 329 0438
Email: info@pinksandbeach.net
www.pinksandbeach.net

CANADA

Pointe Carleton, Quebec
Former keeper's house sleeps 12
Parc national d'Anticosti,
PO Box 179, Port-Menier,
Anticosti, Quebec G0G 2YO
Tel: 418 535 0156
Email: parc.anticosti@sepaq.com

Cape Anguille, Newfoundland
Restored lighthouse keeper's home
Tel: 709 634 2285
Email: info@linkumtours.com
http://linkumtours.com/site/
inns_capeanguille.htm

Cap d'Espoir, Quebec
4 Guest Rooms
Les Maisons du Phare,
92 route du phare, PO Box 249,
Cap d'Espoir, Quebec G0C 1GO
Tel: 418 782 2926
Email:
info@lighthouseaccommodation.com
www.lighthouseaccommodation.com

Cape D'Or, Nova Scotia
Bed and Breakfast
Box 122, Advocate Harbour,
Nova Scotia, Canada B0M 1AO
Tel: 902 670 0534
Email: capedor@hotmail.com
www.capedor.ca

Fort Point, Nova Scotia
Two suites on Lighthouse Route
near to Fort Point Lighthouse
67 Main Street, Liverpool,
Nova Scotia B0T 1KO Canada
Tel: 902 354 6700

Green's Point, New Brunswick
Self-catering cottage, sleeps 5
185 Green's Point Road, L'Etete,
New Brunswick E5C 2N5
Tel: 506 755 3630
Email: letete@nbnet.nb.ca
www.greenspoint.canadianwebs.com

Phare de l'Ile Verte, Quebec
28B Chemin du Phare, Notre Dame
des Sept Douleurs, Quebec
G0L 1KO
Tel: 418 898 2730
Email: phare@ileverte.net
www.ileverte.net/maisonsduphare/
accueil.html

McKay Island, Ontario
PO Box 58, Bruce Mines,
Ontario, Canada POR 1CO

Tel: 705 785 3473 (summer)
Tel: 705 942 0416 (winter)
Email:
brucebaycottages@sympatico.ca
www.brucebaycottages.com

Munroe Point, Nova Scotia
Self-catering cottage
Gordon and Ingrid Boutilier,
CyberRentals
Tel: 902 562 5947
ww.cyberrentals.com/Canada/
vacation-house-Baddeck/p102530.htm

Pleasant Point, Nova Scotia
Pleasant Point Lighthouse on grounds
Seaview Fisherman's
Bed and Breakfast, 99 Kent Road,
Musquodoboit Harbour, Nova Scotia
B0J 2LO Canada
Tel: 902 889 2561

Pointe des Monts, Quebec
Jean-Louis Frenette
   and Eileen Yacyno,
1937 Chemin du Vieux Phare,
Casier Postal 101, Pointe-des-Monts,
Québec Canada GOH 1AO
Tel: 418 939 2332 (summer)
Tel: 418 589 8408 (winter)
Email:
pointe-des-monts@globetrotter.net
www.pointe-des-monts.com

Pot à l'Eau-de-Vie , Quebec
3 room inn.
Overnight stay possible from late May
through mid September.
La Société Duvetnor Ltée,
PO Box 305, 200 rue Hayward,
Rivière-du-Loup,
Québec G5R 3Y9, Canada
Tel: 418 867 1660
Email: informations@duvetnor.com
www.duvetnor.com/en/overnight.htm

Quirpon Island, Newfoundland
Bed and Breakfast
Tel: 709 634 2285
Email: info@linkumtours.com
http://linkumtours.com/site/
inns_quirpon.htm

Swallowtail, New Brunswick
Bed and Breakfast
50 Lighthouse Road,
North Head, Grand Manan,
NB, Canada E5G 2A2
Tel: 506 662 1100
Email:
swallowtailinn_gifts@yahoo.com
www.swallowtailinn.com

Table Head, Quebec
Safari Anticosti Inc, CP 398, Cap-
Chat, Quebec, Canada G0J 1EO
Tel: 418 786 5788
Email: safari@safarianticosti.com

**West Point Lighthouse,
Prince Edward Island**
Bed and Breakfast
PO Box 429, O'Leary,
Prince Edward Island,
COB 1VO Canada
Tel: 902 859 3605
Email: wplight@isn.net
www.westpointlighthouse.com

CROATIA

Adriatica.net, Selska 34,
HR10000, Zagreb, Croatia
Tel: 1 2415 611
Email: info@adriatica.net
www.adriatica.net/lighthouses/
lighthouses_en.htm

Palagruza, Island of Palagruza
Two apartments, each sleeps 4

Plocica, Island of Korcula
Two apartments, sleep 6 and 8

Porer, Pula
Two apartments, each sleeps 4

Prisnjak, Island of Murter
Apartment, sleeps 4

Rt Zub, Porec
Apartment, sleeps 6

Savudrija, Umag
Apartment, sleeps 4

Struga, Island of Lastovo
Four apartments, sleep 2, 3, 4 and 5

Susac, Island of Susac
Two apartments, each sleeps 4

Sv Ivan Na Pucini, Rovinj
Two apartments, each sleeps 4

Sv Petar, Makarska
Apartment, sleeps 4

Veli Rat, Dugi otok
Two apartments, sleep 3 and 4

FINLAND

Bengtskär
Hotel
Wilson Marin and Bengtskär Ltd,
25950 Rosala, Finland
Tel: 2 466 7227
Email: info@bengskar.fi
www.bengtskar.fi

Enskär
Tel: 02 8426 600
Email: matkailu@uusikapunki.fi
www.ulkosaaret.net/docs-fi/
enskar_frames.html

Kylmäpihlaja
Hotel and restaurant
Suvi and Tom Lindqvist
Tel: 44 082 2964
Email: info@kylmapihlaja.com
www.kylmapihlaja.com

Stubben
Tel: 6722 1062

Tankar
Kokkolan Matkailu Oy, Kauppatori
67100 Kokkola
Tel: 8289 402
Email: tourism@kokkola.fi
www.tankar.fi

FRANCE

Fatouville Grestain
Mme Durand, Le Phare,
27210 Fatouville Grestain, France
Tel: 02 32 57 66 56
http://locationhonfleur.com/
FR_detail_chambre.asp?
numeroauto+50

GERMANY

Das Feuerschiff
6 cabins, bar, pub, restaurant
City Sporthafen, Vorsetzen,
20459 Hamburg
Tel: 40 362553/54
Email: lv13@das-feuerschiff.de
www.das-feuerschiff.de

Maritim Strandhotel Travemünde
Navigation light on top of hotel
Trelleborgallee 2, 23570
Lübeck-Travemünde
Tel: 450 2 89 0
Email: info.trv@maritim.de
www.maritim.de

Maritim Strandhotel behind Old Lighthouse Travemünde

Neuwerk Lighthouse
Verein Schullandheim Neuwerk am
Turm, Heinrich-Hertz-Schule Grasweg
72-76, 22303 Hamburg
Tel. 40 46672428
Email:
sa6z220@public.uni-hamburg.de
www.hh.schule.de/hhs/english/
neuweng.htm

Roter Sand
BIS Bremerhaven Touristik,
Tourist Center Hafeninsel,
H H Meier-strasse 6, 27568
Bremerhaven
Tel: 471 9464610
Email: touristik@bis-bremerhaven.de
www.roter-sand.de

IRELAND

Blackhead
*2 self catering cottages,
one sleeps 5, one sleeps 7*
The Irish Landmark Trust, 25 Eustace
Street, Temple Bar, Dublin 2
Tel: 1 670 4773
Email: info@irishlandmark.com
www.irishlandmark.com

Crookhaven
2 self catering cottages,
each sleep 6
Crookhaven Lighthouse, Goleen,
Skibbereen, West Cork
Tel: 353 28 35066

Galley Head
2 self catering cottages,
each sleep 4
The Irish Landmark Trust, 25 Eustace
Street, Temple Bar, Dublin 2
Tel: 1 670 4773
Email: info@irishlandmark.com
www.irishlandmark.com

Loop Head
Self catering cottage, sleeps 5
The Irish Landmark Trust, 25 Eustace
Street, Temple Bar, Dublin 2
Tel: 1 670 4773
Email: info@irishlandmark.com
www.irishlandmark.com

Wicklow Head
Self catering, sleeps 6
Accommodation in disused tower
The Irish Landmark Trust, 25 Eustace
Street, Temple Bar, Dublin 2
Tel: 1 670 4773
Email: info@irishlandmark.com
www.irishlandmark.com

MEXICO

El Faro
Private lighthouse
Hotel, apartments
Calle 10 Norte, Playa del Carmen,
Q Roo 77710 Mexico
Tel: 984 873 0970
Email: elfaro@prodigy.net.mx
www.hotelelfaro.com
www.residenceselfaro.com

NAMIBIA

Shark Island
Namibia Reservations, PO Box 2172,
Otjiwarongo, Namibia
Tel: 264 67 304716
Email: info@namibiareservations.com
www.namibiareservations.com/
sharkislande.html

NETHERLANDS

Harlingen Lighthouse
Dromen aan zee, Postbus 89, 8860
AB Harlingen, Netherlands
Tel: 517 414410
Email: info@dromenaanzee.nl
ww.vuurtoren-harlingen.nl

NEW ZEALAND

The Lighthouse, Wellington
Replica lighthouse,
Bed and breakfast in tower
Bruce Stokell, PO Box 11275,
Wellington, New Zealand
Tel: 472 4177
Email: bruce@thelighthouse.net.nz
www.thelighthouse.net.nz

NORWAY

Buholmråsa, Sør-Trøndelag
Sleeps 10
Saetervik Handel A/S
Tel: 72 57 75 12/15
Email: info@fyropplevelser
www.fyropplevelser.no

Feistein, Rogaland
Six bedrooms in dwelling, sleeps 20
Guests must bring their own food,
drinking water and bedding
Borough of Klepp, Bore Strand
Camping

Tel: 951 39 316
www.fyr.no/fyra/feistein/feistein-e.html

Fyrsteilene
Tel: 67 55 49 90
Email: oslofjf@online.no
www.oslofjordens.friluftsrad.no/
kystleden/Fyrsteilene.html

Geita, Sogn og Fjordane
Nordisk Kunstnersenter Dalsåsen
Tel: 57 73 72 20
Email: stiftnga@jensbua.no
www.fyropplevelser.no

Geitungen
Haugesund Turistforening
Tel: 52 71 53 11
www.lighthouses.no

Grønningen, Vest-Agder
Tel: 38 08 55 66
www.fyr.no/fyra/gronningen/
gronningen-e.html

Guldholmen
Tel: 416 00399
www.guldholmen.no/nyheter/index.php

Hatholmen, Vest-Agder
Tel: 38 27 83 00

Haugjegla, Møre og Romsdal
Hopen aktivitetsgård,
Alf Inge Jenssen, Hopen, 6570,
Smøla, Norway
Tel: 71 54 03 99 / 957 51730
Email: alfinges@online.no
www.hopenaktivitetsgard.no
www.fyropplevelser.no

Hellisøy, Hordaland
Fedje Reiselivsutvikling,
Turistinformasjonen,
5947 Fedje, Norway

Tel: 56 16 43 29 / 56 16 40 48
Email: turist@fedje.org
www.fedje.org

Homborsund, Aust-Agder
Homborsund Lighthouse Management
Tel: 37 04 64 50 / 37 04 30 97
www.lighthouses.no

Kjeungskjaer, Sør-Trøndelag
Mr Joar Birkelund Tel: 72 52 48 87
Or Mr Odd Kalvå Tel: 72 52 10 36
www.lighthouses.no

Kjølnes, Finnmark
Sleeps 15
Ester Utsi / Polmak Gjestegård
Tel: 78 92 89 90 / 481 74 755
Email: info@fyropplevelser.no
www.lighthouses.no
www.fyropplevelser

Kråkenes, Sogn og Fjordane
Bettina Vick and Thomas Bickhardt,
6710 Raudeberg, Norway
Tel: 57 85 55 27
Email: tbickhar@online.no
www.fyropplevelser.no

Landego, Nordland
Skagen Hotell, Bodø
Tel: 75 51 91 00
www.skagen-hotel.no

Lille Presteskjaer, Rogaland
Sleeps 10
Berith Midtbø
Tel: 51 47 72 20 / 909 63 112
Email: berith.midtbo@dabb.no
www.lighthouses.no

Lille Torungen, Aust-Agder
Lille Torungen Foundation
Tel: 37 02 59 25
www.lighthouses.no

Lista, Vest-Agder
Two apartments, each sleeps 7
Tel: 383 97776
Email: post@lista-fyr.com
www.listafyr.com

Litløy
*Carry out manual work at the
lighthouse and stay for free*
Ellen Marie Hansteensen, POB 22,
8469 Bø in Vesteralen, Norway
Tel: 48 09 69 92
Email: kontakt@litloy.no
www.litloy.no

Myken, Nordland
Mrs Gro Bygdevoll,
Myken Fyr, 8199 Myken, Norway
Tel: 75 09 60 28 / 75 09 60 20
Email: eilero@online.no
www.www.myken.no

Obrestad, Rogaland
Hå gamle prestegard
4365 Naerbo, Norway
Tel: 51 79 16 60 / 51 79 30 00
Email: kultur@ha.kommune.no
www.fyropplevelser.no

Runde, Møre og Romsdal
Ålesund og Sunmøre Turisforening
Tel: 70 12 58 04
www.lighthouses.no

Ryvarden, Hordaland
Tel: 53 74 80 00
Email:
postmottak@sveio.kommune.no
www.lighthouses.no

Ryvingen, Vest-Agder
Ryvingens Venner,
Rita Dyrstad
Tel: 38 26 87 16
www.lighthouses.no

Skongenes, Sogn og Fjordane
Britt Småvik
Tel: 57 85 45 64
Email: b_sk@msn.com
www.fyropplevelser.no

Slåtterøy, Hordaland
Friends of Slåtterøy Lighthouse
Tel: 974 97 666 / 907 95 673
Email: e-melin@online.no
www.lighthouses.no

Slettnes, Finnmark
Fyropplevelser,
Postboks 487,
6067 Ulsteinvik, Norway
Tel: 48 04 08 20 / 922 39 777
Email: info@fyropplevelser.no
Email: slettnesfyr@hotmail.com
www.fyropplevelser.no

Songvår, Vest-Agder
Søgne Municipality
Tel: 38 05 55 55
www.fyr.no/fyra/songvar/
songvar-e.html

Strømtangen, Østfold
Onsøbeviset, v/Bjørn Enger,
Marnetveien 29, 1621 Gressvik
Tel: 988 77 640
Email: engerbj@online.no
www.stromtangen.com

Struten, Østfold
Tel: 693 40381 / 693 40381
Email: struten@start.no
http://home.no.net/struten/

Svenner, Vestfold
Westfold County
Coastal Association
Tel: 91 37 05 70
www.svenner.info

Tranøy, Nordland
Tranøy Fyr Kystopplevelser A/S
Tel: 913 28 013
Email: info@tranoyfyr.no
http://en.tranoyfyr.no
www.fyropplevelser.no

Ulla, Møre og Romsdal
Kystverkklubben Midt-Norge
Tel: 905 005 16 / 958 30438
Email: info@fyropplevelser.no
www.fyropplevelser.no

Ulvesund, Sogn og Fjordane
Tel: 57 85 17 77 / 952 40487
Email: ulvesundfyr@start.no
http://booking.nordfjord.no
www.fyropplevelser.no

Utsire, Rogaland
Arna Leidland
or Arnstein Eeek
Tel: 52 75 01 00
Email: arna@utsira.kommune.no
or arnstein@utsira.konnune.no
www.utsira.kommune.no/
Kulture_og_fritid/kunstnerleilighet/view

Vardø, Finnmark
Tel: 78 98 69 07
Email: info@fyropplevelser.no
www.fyropplevelser.no

Vikeholmen, Rogaland
Skudenes Tourist Office
Tel: 52 82 72 22
www.fyr.no/fyra/vikeholmen/
vikeholmen-e.html

SOUTH AFRICA

Cape Columbine,
Western Cape Coast
Two self catering cottages, each
sleeps 6

Central Reservation Office
Tel: 21 449 2400
Email: lighthouse.tourism@transnet.net
www.transnetnationalportsauthority.net/
NPA_lighthouse_Cape_Columbine.html

Cape St Blaize,
Western Cape Coast
Self-catering cottage, sleeps 6
Central Reservation Office
Tel: 21 449 2400
Email: lighthouse.tourism@transnet.net
www.transnetnationalportsauthority.net/
NPA_lighthouse_Cape_St_Blaize.html

Danger Point,
Western Cape Coast
Self-catering cottage,
sleeps 4
Central Reservation Office
Tel: 21 449 2400
Email: lighthouse.tourism@transnet.net
www.transnetnationalportsauthority.net/
NPA_lighthouse_danger_point.html

Great Fish Point,
Eastern Cape Coast
Two self-catering cottages,
each sleeps 6
Central Reservation Office
Tel: 21 449 2400
Email: lighthouse.tourism@transnet.net
www.transnetnationalportsauthority.net/
NPA_lighthouse_Great_Fish_Point.html

North Sand Bluff,
Kwazulu-Natal
Two self-catering cottages,
each sleeps 4
Central Reservations Office
Tel: 082 374 4114
Email: info@kzncoast.co.za
www.transnetnationalportsauthority.net/
NPA_lighthouse_North_Sand_
Bluff.html

SOUTH KOREA

Gadeokdo Lighthouse
Busan Regional Maritime Affairs
and Fisheries Office
Tel: 051 609 6546 / 7

SWEDEN

Bergudden
Hostel
Birgitta Fritzdotter
Tel: 705 559023, 768 27946
Email: holmon.hembygd@home.se
www.holmon.com/hembygd

Bjuröklubb
Café and Lodging
930 10 Lövånger
Tel: 913 32211, 705 106660
Email: arena@bjuroklubb.se
www.bjuroklubb.se

Dämman
Hotel
The WaterHotel,
Box 152,
SE-383, 24 Mönsterås
Tel: 499 42 041, 708 256483
Email: info@waterhotel.com
www.waterhotel.com

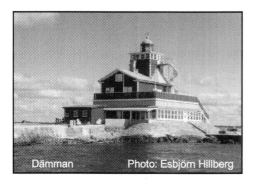
Dämman   Photo: Esbjörn Hillberg

Djurö
Hostel
Tel: 708 256482, 708 256483
www.naturvardsverket.se

Djursten
Hostel, apartment, café
Tel: 173 333 10
Email: kafe@djursten.com
www.djursten.com

Femörehuvud
Apartment
Tel: 155 38170
www.oxelosund.se

Garpen
Kungsvägen 41,
385 40 Bergkvara
Tel: 486 20437
Email: turistbyran@torsas.se
www.garpen.se

Gotska Sandön
Hostel
Tel: 498 240450, 708 225918
Email: info@resestugan.se
www.gotskasandon.se

Gran
Primitive lodge
Tel: 652 16175
www.bokningscentralen.com

Hallands Väderö
Hostel and apartment
Tel: 431 366194, 431 363283
Email: info@vaderotrafiken.se
www.vaderotrafiken.se
www.vaderotrafiken.se

Häradskär
Hostel
Tel: 734 321258, 707 966161

128

Högbonden
Hostel
Kajsa and Ove Grandics
Tel: 613 230 05 or 613 231 00 (winter)
www.hogbonden.se

Hållö
Hostel and conference centre
Lena Stranne
Tel: 523 303 17, 703 536822
Email: info@utpost-hallo.nu
www.utpost-hallo.nu

Hanö
Hostel, apartment
and conference centre
Tel: 456 53000, 456 53084
www.hano.nu

Huvudskär
Hostel
Tel: 8 501 50800
www.dalaro.org

Landsort
Bed and Breakfast, Hotel
Tel: 8 520 34005, 8 5203 4111
Email: vandrarhemmet@landsort.com
www.landsort.com
www.landsort.nu

Nidingen
Hostel and conference centre
Tel: 70 670 90 89
Email: calle@nidingen.se
www.nidingen.se

Örskär
Hostel
Siv Ölund and Per Mattsson
Örskärs Fyrplats,
740 71 Öregrund
Tel: 173 340 21, 708 339256
Email: orskars.vandrarhem@telia.com
www.orskars-fyr.se

Niding — Photo: Esbjörn Hillberg

Pater Noster
Hostel, restaurant
and conference centre
Tel: 737 000814
www.kurstpaternoster.se

Rödkallen
Hotel and restaurant
Fyrhotellet Hällvägen 10,
97251 Luleå
Tel: 920 257750, 705 493642
Email: info@fyrhotellet.com
www.fyrhotellet.com

Segerstad
Hostel, apartment
Tel: 485 664 062, 709 666450
Email: Christian@Segerstadsfyr.se
www.segerstadsfyr.se

Smygehuk
Hostel
Tel: 410 24583
Email: info@sfturist.se
www.smygehukhostel.com

Söderarm
Hotel, restaurant
and conference centre
Tjockö PL 105, S-760 15 Gräddö
Tel: 176 43212, 703 265833
Email: info@soderarm.com
www.soderarm.com

Stångudden, Lurö
Hostel
Tel: 533 29012
Tel: 705 216733
www.luringen.se

Stora Fjäderägg   Photo: Esbjörn Hillberg

Stora Fjäderägg
Hostel
Tel: 90 49201, 90 55220
Email: logi@fyrvaktaren.se
www.fyrvaktaren.se

Stora Karlsö
Hostel, restaurant
Karlsö Jagt &
Djurskyddförenings AB,
Box 1431, 621 25 Visby
Tel: 498 240450
Tel: 498 240500
Email: boka@storakarlso.se
www.storakarlso.se

Storjungfrun
Cottages
Tel: 270 75353
www.soderhamn.com

Utklippan
Hostel
Svenska Kryssarklubben
Tel: 702 18727,
Tel: 455 303490
www.karlskrona.se

Vinga
Lodging, café
Tel: 31 858000,
Tel: 31 489027
www.wingavanner.se

UNITED STATES OF AMERICA

Bass River, Massachussetts
Bed & Breakfast and cottages
Mr and Mrs Stone, The Lighthouse
Inn, Lighthouse Inn Road,
Box 128, West Dennis on Cape Cod,
Massachusetts 02670
Tel: 508 398 2244
www.lighthouse.cc/bassriver

Big Bay Point, Michigan
Bed & Breakfast
3 Lighthouse Road, Big Bay,
Michigan 49808
Tel: 906 345 9957
Email:
keepers@bigbaylighthouse.com
www.bigbaylighthouse.com

Big Sable Point, Michigan
Live and work at the lighthouse
for two weeks
Big Sable Point Lighthouse Keepers
Association, PO Box 673, Ludington,
Michigan 49431
Tel: 231 845 7343
www.bigsablelighthouse.org

Browns Point, Washington
Become a lighthouse keeper
for one week's duty
Points NE Historical Society,
1000 Town Center,
Suite 180,
PMB 135 Browns Point,
Washington 98422
Tel: 253 927 2536
www.pointsnortheast.org/cottage.html

De Tour Reef, Michigan
Become a keeper for a few days
DRLPS Lighthouse Keeper Program,
PO Box 307, Drummond Island,
Michigan 49726
Tel: 906 493 6609
Email: keepers@drlps.com
www.drlps.com

Door County Lighthouse Inn, Wisconsin
Replica Lighthouse, Bed and Breakfast, Lighthouse Tours
Claire and Frank Murphy,
4639 Orchard Road, PO Box 165,
Egg Harbor, Wisconsin 54209
Tel: 920 868 9088
Email: info@dclighthouseinn.com
www.dclighthouseinn.com

Door County Lighthouse Inn
Photo: Claire and Frank Murphy

East Brother, California
Bed & Breakfast
East Brother Light Station, 117 Park
Place, Point Richmond, CA 94801
Tel: 510 233 2385
Email: info@ebls.org
www.ebls.org

Faro Blanco, Florida
Privately built lighthouse.
Faro Blanco Marine Resort,
1966 Overseas Highway, Marathon,
Florida 33050
Tel: 305 743 9018

First Light, Maine
Replica lighthouse, Bed and Breakfast
Beverly Bartlett, First Light Bed &
Breakfast, 821 East Blue Hill Road,
Blue Hill, Maine 04614
Tel: 207 374 5879
Email: info@firstlightbandb.com
www.firstlightbandb.com

Grand Traverse, Michigan
Become a keeper for a week
Grand Traverse Lighthouse Museum,
PO Box 43, 15500 N Lighthouse Pt
Road, Northport, Michigan 49670
Tel: 231 386 7195
Email: gtlthse@triton.net
www.grandtraverselighthouse.com

Heceta Head, Oregon
Bed and Breakfast
Michelle and Steven Bursey, Mike and
Carol Korgan, 92072 Highway 101
South, Yachats, Oregon 97498
Tel: 866 547 3696
Email:keepers@hecetalighthouse.com
www.hecetalighthouse.com

Isle Au Haut, Maine
Bed & Breakfast,
Self-catering cottage
Jeff and Judi Burke,
Robinson Point Lighthouse Station,
PO Box 26, Isle Au Haut, Maine 04645
Tel: 207 460 0257
Email: inn@keepershouse.com
www.keepershouse.com

Jacobsville, Michigan
Bed and Breakfast
Jacobsville Lighthouse Inn,
Michigan
Tel: 906 523 4137
Email: mditty23@netzero.com
www.jacobsvillelighthouse.com

Katie's Light, Florida
Replica lighthouse
98 South Fletcher Avenue,
Amelia Island, Florida 32034
Tel: 904 277 4851
Email: info@ameliaislandvacation.com
www.ameliaislandvacation.com/
katieslight.html

Lighthouse Inn, Wisconsin
Hotel, Two Rivers Lighthouse
Lighthouse Inn,
1515 Memorial Drive,
Highway 42, Two Rivers,
Wisconsin 54241
Tel: 920 793 4524
Email: rooms@lhinn.com
www.lhinn.com

Little River, Maine
Self-catering
PO Box 671, East Machias,
Maine 04630
Tel: 207 259 3833
Email: LittleRiverLight@
LighthouseFoundation.org
www.littleriverlight.org

Monomoy Point, Massachusetts
Wikis Way, Morris Island, Chatham,
Massachusetts 02633
Tel: 508 945 0594
Email: fw5rw_mnwr@fws.gov
www.lighthouse.cc/monomoy

New Dungeness, Washington
Become a Lighthouse Keeper.
Available only to members of New
Dungeness Light Station
New Dungeness
Light Station Association,
PO Box 1283,
Sequim, Washington 98382
Tel: 360 683 9166

Email: lightkeepers@
newdungenesslighthouse.com
www.newdungenesslighthouse.com

North Head, Washington
Self-catering, two nights minimum stay
Ilwaco, Washington State Parks
Tel: 800 360 4240
Email: reservations@parks.wa.gov
www.parks.wa.gov/vacationhouses/
capedisappointment.asp

Odiak Pharos, Alaska
Privately built lighthouse on a barge
Bed and breakfast
Cordova Rose Lodge, 1315 Whitshed
Box 1494, Cordova, Alaska 99574
Tel: 907 424 7673
Email: info@cordovarose.com
www.cordovarose.com

Pigeon Point, California
Hostel
210 Pigeon Point Road, Highway 1,
Pescadero, California 94060-9713
Tel: 650 879 0633
Email: info@norcalhostels.org
www.norcalhostels.org/pigeon

Point Arena, California
Self-catering,
Guided tours of the lighthouse
Point Arena Lighthouse Keepers,
PO Box 11, 45500 Lighthouse Road,
Point Arena, California 95468
Tel: 877 725 4448
Email: palight@mcn.org
www.pointarenalighthouse.com

Point Cabrillo, California
Bed and Breakfast
Lighthouse Inn at Point Cabrillo,
45300 Lighthouse Road, PO Box 461
Mendocino, California 95460

Tel: 707 937 6124
www.pointcabrillo.org

Point Montara, California
Hostel
PO Box 737, Montara,
California 94037
Tel: 650 728 7177
Email: info@norcalhostels.org
www.norcalhostels.org/montara/

Point Robinson, Washington
Two self-catering cottages,
sleep 4 and 6
Tel: 206 463 9602
Email:cynthia@vashonparkdistrict.org
www.vashonparkdistrict.org/
keepers.htm

Race Point, Massachusetts
Bed and Breakfast,
Self-catering cottage
PO Box 570, North Truro,
Massachusetts 02652
Tel: 508 487 9930
Email:
racepointlighthouse@comcast.net
www.racepointlighthouse.net

Rockwell, Alaska
Bed and Breakfast
1309 Halibut Point Road,
Sitka, Alaska 99835
Tel: 907 747 3056

Rose Island, Rhode Island
Become a keeper for a week
Rose Island Lighthouse Foundation,
PO Box 1419,
Newport,
Rhode Island 02840
Tel: 401 847 4242
Email: keeper@roseisland.org
www.roseislandlighthouse.org

Sand Hills, Michigan
Bed and Breakfast
Mr Bill Frabotta, Keeper,
Sand Hills Lighthouse, Five Mile Point
Road, PO Box 298, Ahmeek ,
Michigan 49901
Tel: 906 337 1744
www.sandhillslighthouseinn.com

Saugerties, New York
Bed and Breakfast, public tours
Saugerties Lighthouse,
168 Lighthouse Drive,
New York 12477
Tel: 845 247 0656
Email: info@saugertieslighthouse.com
www.saugertieslighthouse.com

Selkirk Lighthouse

Selkirk, New York
Self catering
Selkirk Lighthouse, 6 Lake Road
Extension, PO Box 228, Pulaski,
New York 13142-0228
Tel: 315 298 6688
Email: selkirklight@hotmail.com
http://people.maine.com/lights/
reserve.htm

Sentinel Island, Alaska
Self-catering. Transportation to
island by helicopter or boat.
Gastineau Channel Historical Society,
1001 Basin Road, Juneau,
Alaska 99801
Tel: 907 586 5338
Email: glrrlg@alaska.net

Sharps Point, Maryland
Bed and Breakfast.
Private aid to navigation.
Janice and William Costello,
Chesapeake Bay Lighthouse
Bed and Breakfast,
1423 Sharps Point Road,
Annapolis, Maryland 21401
Tel: 410 757 0248
www.travelassist.com/reg/md101s.html

Smithfield Station, Virginia
Hotel. Replica lighthouse with suites
415 South Church Street, PO Box 486,
Smithfield, Virginia 23431
Tel: 757 357 7700
Email:
smithfieldstation@smithfieldstation.com
www.smithfieldstation.com

Thacher Island, Massachusetts
PO Box 73, Rockport,
Massachusetts 01966
Tel: 617 599 2590
Email: info@thacherisland.org
www.thacherisland.org

Thirty Mile Point, New York
Self-catering, sleeps 6
Golden Hill State Park,
9691 Lower Lake Road,
Barker, New York 14102
Tel: 716 795 3885
www.reserveamerica.com

Tibbetts Point, New York
Hostel
Tibbetts Point Lighthouse Hostel,
33439 Country Route 6,
Cape Vincent,
New York 13618-3174
Tel: 315 654 3450
Email: lighthousehostel@tds.net
www.hiusa.org

Thirty Mile Point

Two Harbors, Minnesota
Bed and Breakfast
Lighthouse Bed and Breakfast,
1 Lighthouse Point, PO Box 128
Two Harbors, Minnesota 55616
Tel: 218 834 4814
Email: lakehist@lakenet.com
www.lighthousebb.org

Valleyview, Iowa
Bed and breakfast
15931 Lore Mound Road,
Dubuque 52002, Iowa USA
Tel: 563 583 7327
Email:
innkeeper@lighthousevalleyview.com

Whitefish Point, Michigan
Bed and Breakfast
18335 N Whitefish Point Road,
Paradise, Michigan 49768
Tel: 888 492 3747
www.shipwreckmuseum.org

Wings Neck, Massachusetts
Christina Stevens,
PO Box 694, South Chatham,
Massachusetts 02659
Tel: 508 430 8685
Email:
admin@wingsnecklighthouse.com
www.wingsnecklighthouse.com

APPENDIX 2:
UK VISITOR CENTRES AND MUSEUMS
WITH LIGHTHOUSE-RELATED MATERIAL

Please note: Visitor centres may be open for limited periods only, and may not be open throughout the year. Visitors are strongly advised to check opening times beforehand to avoid disappointment.

SOUTH WEST ENGLAND

Lizard Lighthouse, Cornwall
Visitor centre and accommodation.
Tel: 01326 290202
Email: lighthouselizard@aol.com
www.trinityhouse.co.uk

Smeaton's Tower, Plymouth

Smeaton's Tower, Plymouth, Devon
Fourth Eddystone Lighthouse located on Plymouth Hoe.
Tel: 01752 304774
Email: museum@plymouth.gov.uk
www.plymouth.gov.uk

Start Point Lighthouse, Devon
Visitor centre and accommodation.
Tel: 01803 770606
www.trinityhouse.co.uk

SOUTHERN ENGLAND

Portland Bill Lighthouse, Dorset
Visitor centre.
Tel: 01305 820495
Tel: 01255 245011
www.trinityhouse.co.uk

Anvil Point Lighthouse, Dorset
Visitor centre and accommodation.
Tel: 01255 245011
Email: chris.dodson@thls.org
www.trinityhouse.co.uk

Hurst Castle, Hampshire
Visitor Centre, including Trinity House and ALK Room. Note: lighthouses are not open to the public.
Tel: 01590 642344
www.hurstcastle.co.uk

Haslar Lightvessel, Hampshire
Mary Mouse no2 Bar and Bistro.
Haslar Marina, Haslar Road, Gosport, Hants PO12 1NU
Tel: 023 9260 1201
Email: sales@haslarmarina.co.uk
www.haslarmarina.co.uk

St Catherine's Lighthouse, IOW
Visitor centre and accommodation.
Tel: 01983 855069
www.trinityhouse.co.uk

St Catherine's Oratory, Isle of Wight
14th century oratory, originally used as a lighthouse. On view at all times.
www.english-heritage.org.uk

Alderney Lighthouse, Channel Islands
Visitor centre.
Tel: 01481 823077
www.trinityhouse.co.uk

Dungeness Old Lighthouse, Kent
Visitor centre
Romney Marsh, Kent TN29 9NB
Tel: 01797 321300
Email:info@dungenesslighthouse.com
www.dungenesslighthouse.com

Roman Pharos, Kent
In grounds of Dover Castle.
Tel: 01304 201628/211067
www.english-heritage.org.uk

South Foreland Lighthouse, Kent
Visitor centre and accommodation.
St Margaret's Bay, Dover,
Kent CT15 6HP
Tel: 01304 852463
www.nationaltrust.org.uk

Greenwich Maritime Museum, London
Tarbat ness optic, maritime library.
Greenwich, London SE10 9NF
Tel: 020 8858 4422 / 020 8312 6565
www.nmm.ac.uk

Trinity Buoy Wharf, London
Former Trinity House training centre, and engineering depot. Now a site for artistic and cultural activities.
Urban Space Management Ltd
The Riverside Building,
Trinity Buoy Wharf,
64 Orchard Place, London E14 0JW
Tel: 020 7515 7153
Email:
sarah.hewson@urban-space.co.uk
www.trinitybuoywharf.com

Trinity Buoy Wharf, London

EAST ANGLIA

Harwich High Light, Essex
National Vintage Wireless Museum.
Tony O'Neil, West Street,
Harwich CO12 3DQ
Tel: 01206 322606
www.nvwm.freeservers.com

Harwich Low Light, Essex
Maritime Museum in former Low Light.
Mr A Rutter, Harbour Crescent,
Harwich, Essex CO12 3NJ
Tel: 01225 503429
Email: info@harwich-society.com
www.harwich.net/society.htm

Southwold Lighthouse, Suffolk
Visitor centre.
Tel: 01502 722576
www.trinityhouse.co.uk

Lowestoft Maritime Museum
Whapload Road, Lowestoft, Suffolk
Tel: 01502 561963

Happisburgh Lighthouse, Norfolk
The UK's only independently run operational lighthouse.
Carol Palfrey, Solar Via,
Happisburgh, Norfolk NR12 0QU
Tel: 01692 650442
Email: Happislight@keme.co.uk
www.happisburgh.org

NORTH EAST ENGLAND

Spurn Lightship,
East Riding of Yorkshire
Ferens Art Gallery, Queen Victoria
Square, Kingston-upon-Hull HU1 3RA
Tel: 01482 613902
www.hullcc.gov.uk

Withernsea Lighthouse,
East Riding of Yorkshire
Visitor centre Hull Road, Withernsea,
East Yorkshire HU19 2DY
Tel: 01964 614834
Email:withernsealighthouse@fsmail.net
www.withernsealighthouse.co.uk

Flamborough Head Lighthouse,
East Riding of Yorkshire
Visitor centre.
Tel: 01262 673769
Email: sewerby.hall@eastriding.gov.uk
www.trinityhouse.co.uk

Whitby Harbour Light, West Pier
North Yorkshire
Langborne Road,Whitby, YO21 1YN
Tel: 01947 602674

Souter Lighthouse,
Tyne and Wear
Visitor centre and accommodation
Souter Lighthouse, Coast Road,
Whitburn, Sunderland
Tel: 0191 529 3161
www.nationaltrust.org.uk

Trinity Maritime Centre,
Tyne and Wear
Broad Chare, Quayside,
Newcastle upon Tyne NE1 3DQ
Tel: 0191 232 8226
Email:
info@trinityhousenewcastle.org.uk
www.trinityhousenewcastle.org.uk

St Mary's Lighthouse,
Tyne and Wear
Visitor centre.
Access dependent on tide times.
St Mary's Island, Whitley Bay,
Tyne and Wear NE26 4RS
Tel: 0191 200 8650
Email:
info@friendsofstmarysisland.co.uk
www.friendsofstmarysisland.co.uk

St Mary's Lighthouse

Grace Darling Museum,
Northumberland
Radcliffe Road, Bamburgh,
Northumberland NE69 7AE
Tel: 01668 214910
www.rnli.org.uk/who_we_are/
the_heritage_trust/
grace_darling_museum

Longstone Lighthouse,
Northumberland
Tel: 01665 721210
Tel: 01655 721819
www.farneislandboattrips.co.uk

NORTH WEST ENGLAND

Sir John Barrow Memorial,
Ulverston, Cumbria
Lighthouse monument on Hoad Hill
dedicated to Sir John Barrow,
Secretary to the Admiralty and founder
of the Royal Geographic Society.

Merseyside Maritime Museum, Liverpool, Merseyside
Albert Dock, Liverpool L3 4AQ
Tel: 0151 478 4499
www.liverpoolmuseums.org.uk/maritime

Leasowe Lighthouse, Wirral
Friends of Leasowe Lighthouse,
Leasowe Common, Moreton,
Wirral CH46 4TA
Tel: 0151 678 5488
Email: info@leasowelighthouse.co.uk
www.leasowelighthouse.co.uk

SCOTLAND EAST COAST

National Museum of Scotland, Edinburgh
*Eilean Glas, Sule Skerry
and Inchkeith optics*
Chambers Street,
Edinburgh, EH1 1JF
Tel: 0131 225 7534
www.nms.ac.uk

North Carr Lightship, Dundee
*Currently moored in Dundee Harbour.
Not open to the public.*
www.northcarr.org.uk

Arbroath Signal Tower, Angus
*Former signal tower for
Bell Rock Lighthouse.
Bell Rock display.*
Signal Tower, Ladyloan,
Arbroath DD1 1PU
Tel: 01241 875598
Email: signal.tower@angus.gov.uk

Aberdeen Maritime Museum
Rattray Head optic.
Shiprow, Aberdeen, AB11 5BY
Tel: 01224 337700
www.aagm.co.uk

Museum of Scottish Lighthouses, Fraserburgh, Aberdeenshire
Kinnaird Head, Stevenson Road,
Fraserburgh AB43 9DU
Tel: 01346 511022
Email:info@lighthousemuseum.org.uk
www.lighthousemuseum.org.uk

Lossiemouth Fisheries Museum, Moray
Covesea Skerries optic on display.
Pitgaveny Street,
Lossiemouth IV31
Tel: 01343 813772

Wick Heritage Centre, Highland
Noss Head optic on display.
18-27 Bank Row, Wick, KW1 5EY
Tel: 01955 605393
www.wickheritage.org
Email: museum@wickheritage.org

ORKNEY AND SHETLAND

Stromness Museum, Orkney
*Exhibition on Orkney lighthouses
and keepers and their families,
Hoy Low optic.*
52 Alfred Street,
Stromness, Orkney
Tel: 01856 850025
www.orkney.org/museums/stromness.htm

North Ronaldsay, Orkney
New lighthouse and old beacon.
Tours of new lighthouse by
appointment only.
William Muir, North Ronaldsay Trust
Hooking, North Ronaldsay, Orkney
KW17 2BE
Tel: 01857 633257
Email: nrt@orkneycommunities.co.uk

Bressay Lighthouse, Shetland
Visitor centre and accommodation.
Shetland Amenity Trust, Garthspool,
Lerwick, Shetland ZE1 0NY
Tel: 01595 694688
Email:
shetamenity.trust@zetnet.co.uk
www.lighthouse-holidays.com

SCOTLAND WEST COAST

Gairloch Heritage Museum,
Highland
Rua Reidh optic and fog horn.
Achtercairn, Gairloch, IV21 2BP
Tel: 01445 712287
Email:
info@gairlochheritagemuseum.org.uk
www.gairlochheritagemuseum.org.uk

Ardnamurchan Lighthouse,
Highland
Visitor centre and accommodation.
Ardnamurchan Lighthouse Trust,
Kilchoan, Acharacle Argyll PH36 4LN
Tel: 01972 510210
www.ardnamurchan.u-net.com

Hynish Signal Tower, Tiree
Skerryvore Lighthouse Museum.
North Parade Chambers,
75A Banbury Road, Oxford OX2 6PE
Tel: 01865 311468
Email: info@hebrideantrust.org
ww.hebrideantrust.org

Mull of Galloway Lighthouse
Visitor centre and accommodation
South Rhins Development Trust,
Stoneykirk Community Hall,
Stoneykirk, Stranraer DG9 9DG
Tel: 01776 830682
Email: info@mull-of-galloway.co.uk
www.mull-of-galloway.co.uk

WALES

Great Orme Visitor Centre,
Llandudno
Great Orme's Head optic.
www.greatorme.org.uk

South Stack Lighthouse, Anglesey
Tel: 01248 724444 or 01407 763207
www.trinityhouse.co.uk

Helwick Lightship, Swansea
Ex Trinity House LV91
National Waterfront Museum,
Oystermouth Road, Maritime Quarter,
Swansea SA1 3RD
Tel: 01792 638950
www.museumwales.ac.uk/en/
swansea

Nash Point Lighthouse, Glamorgan
Visitor centre
Tel: 01255 245011 (Chris Dodson)
Email chris.dodson@thls.org
Tel: 07906 469168 (Chris Williams)
Email: chris@coastalribtours.co.uk
www.trinityhouse.co.uk

Goleulong 2000 Lightship, Cardiff
Ex Trinity House LV14.
Christian Centre with café.
Waterfront Park, Harbour Drive,
Cardiff Bay CF10 4PA
Tel: 029 2048 7609
Email: admin@lightship2000.org.uk
www.lightship2000.co.uk

USEFUL ADDRESSES

UNITED KINGDOM

Association of Lighthouse Keepers
Membership open to everyone with an interest in lighthouses and lightvessels

Sallyann Anderson,
Membership Secretary,
29 Kingsmead, Abbeymead,
Gloucester GL4 5DY
Tel: 01452 371622
Email: membership@alk.org.uk
www.alk.org.uk

Friends of Happisburgh Lighthouse
Supporting the UK's only independently run working lighthouse

Carol Palfrey,
"Solar Via", Happisburgh
Norwich NR12 0QU
Tel: 01692 650442
Email: happislight.keme.co.uk
www.happisburgh.org

Maritime Heritage Tours
Tour operator specialising in tailor – made lighthouse and maritime tours for groups

Michael Walter, Seaways,
1 Albert House, Albert Street,
Ventnor, Isle of Wight PO38 1JG
Tel: 01983 855069
Email: maritimelights@talktalk.net

Trinity House
General Lighthouse Authority for England, Wales and Channel Islands

Tower Hill, London EC3N 4DH
Tel: 020 7481 6900

Harwich Depot
The Quay, Harwich,
Essex CO12 3JW
Tel: 01255 245000

Email: enquiries@thls.org
www.trinityhouse.co.uk

Northern Lighthouse Board
General Lighthouse Authority for Scotland and the Isle of Man

84 George Street,
Edinburgh EH2 3DA
Tel: 0131 473 3100
Email: enquiries@nlb.org.uk
www.nlb.org.uk

IRELAND

Commissioners of Irish Lights
General Lighthouse Authority for Northern and Republic of Ireland

Harbour Road, Dun Laoghaire,
Co Dublin
Tel: 353 (0) 1 2715400
Email: info@cil.ie
www.cil.ie

AUSTRALIA

Lighthouses of Australia Inc
PO Box 4734, Knox City,
VIC 3152 Australia
Email: keeper@lighthouse.net.au
www.lighthouse.net.au

FINLAND

Finlands Fyrsällskap
The Finnish Lighthouse Society

Vihdintie 13 B 5, 00320 Helsinki
Tel: 040 860 1649
Email: info@majakkaseura.fi
www.majakkaseura.fi/eng/society

GERMANY

Leuchtfeuer
Magazine, published in German

Klaus Kern, Pestalozzitrasse 28,
65428 Rüsselheim
Tel: 6142 81607
Email:
Klaus.kern@leuchtfeuer-magazin.de
www.leuchtfeuer-magazin.de

NETHERLANDS

Nederlandse Vuurtoren Vereniging
Dutch Lighthouse Society

Email: secretaris@vuurtorens.org
www.vuurtorens.org

NORWAY

Norsk Fyrhistorisk Forening
Norwegian Lighthouse Society

Email: webmaster@fyr.no
www.lighthouses.no

SWEDEN

Svenska Fyrsällskapet
Swedish Lighthouse Society

Esbjörn Hillberg, Hus 154, Donsö
Backe 16, S-430 82 Donsö Sweden
Email: esbjorn@hillberg.com
www.fyr.org

USA

Lighthouse Depot
Lighthouse Store

PO Box 1690, Wells, Maine 04090
www.lighthousedepot.com

Lighthouse Digest Magazine

PO Box 250, East Machias,
Maine 04630
Tel: 207 259 2121
Email: editor@lhdigest.com
www.lhdigest.com

US Lighthouse Society

244 Kearny Street, San Francisco, CA
94108 USA
Tel: 415 362 7255
Email: info@uslhs.org
www.uslhs.org

WORLDWIDE

World Lighthouse Society

Email: wls@worldlighthouses.org
www.worldlighthouses.org

INDEX